Steigenberger The Cookbook

Christine Steigenberger   Mike Meyer-Ditandy

Content

Content

Content

All recipes are for four people. Ingredients and serving methods have been designed for any amateur cook to follow with ease. The recommended wines and drinks have been selected in cooperation with the Vox Hospitalitatis company (www.voxhos.de), Horst Georg Wende, Oestrich-Winkel.

Foreword

Good food is never simply good food. More an experience that addresses all the senses, that inspires us and leads us to ever new worlds. A pleasure best shared with friends and family. Unusual restaurants and joy in every treat from kitchen or cellar have been the fundamental principles ever since the Steigenberger Hotels were founded by Albert Steigenberger in 1930. The restaurants are a crucial element part of our hotels, intended to spoil the guest with unusual culinary delights. And the ambience and service must harmonise as perfectly as the menus and wines.

This year, the Steigenberger Hotel Company is celebrating its 75th anniversary. A splendid reason for presenting the culinary expertise of Steigenberger cooks, their quality, their in-depth knowledge of wine and food and their ability to innovate – all in a very unusual cookbook. The result is now in your hands. The 34 chefs from our hotels in Germany, Austria, Switzerland, the Netherlands and Egypt have all come together to reveal their favourite recipes. We, too, have taken great pleasure in adding our own favourites. The outcome is a fine culinarium where international meets regional, where plain meets exotic and where innovation meets tradition.

Throughout his entire life, Egon Steigenberger's dearest wish was to publish a cookbook together with his top Steigenberger chefs. He would have been delighted to cooperate on this book. He owned an impressive collection of cookbooks garnered from every corner of the world, which he constantly augmented. In this, our anniversary year, we have finally made his wish come true.

We hope our Steigenberger Cookbook succeeds in beguiling you with the Steigenberger philosophy and expertise in food and drink.

Anne-Marie Steigenberger   *Bettina Steigenberger*

Christine Steigenberger   *Claudia Steigenberger*

Anne-Marie Steigenberger

Ingredients

Stuffed
Courgettes

Involtini
with green Asparagus
in Cep-Mushroom Gravy

Apple Soufflé

Involtini

20 g dried cep mushrooms

300 g green asparagus

4 thin slices of veal (topside)

salt, pepper

2 tbsp coarse-grain mustard

4 large slices of air-curd ham

4 shallots, finely diced

2 tbsp oil for browning

1 tbsp tomato purée

150 ml rosé wine

500 ml beef stock (see glossary)

1 tbsp food starch

2 tbsp port

1 tbsp cold butter

Sachsenhäuser Apple Soufflé

50 g butter for greasing; 2 tbsp sugar for sprinkling; 4 tart apples,
peeled and cut into thin slices; 80 g sultanas; 2 tbsp rum; 300 g brioche; 250 ml milk;
250 ml cream; 6 eggs; 70 g sugar; 2 vanilla pods; icing sugar

Grease a large, heat-proof baking dish and sprinkle with sugar. Put sultanas in a sieve and rinse under hot water, dry well and, together with the rum, mix with the apples. Cut the brioche into approx. 1 cm thick slices. Use half of these to line the dish, spread on the apple-sultana mix, finishing with the remaining brioche slices. Thoroughly beat milk, cream, eggs and sugar in a dish and pass through a strainer, then stir in the scraped out vanilla pulp. Pour the mix over the brioche slices in the dish, place baking dish on the lowest shelf of the oven and bake at 220°C for approx. 15 minutes. Once the 15 minutes are up, reduce the temperature to 170°C and bake for a further 25 minutes. Dust apple soufflé with icing sugar and serve warm.

Preparation Dessert

**Bettina
Steigenberger**

Lasagne of marinated Salmon
on Potato Fritters

Red Mullet
on Leek Risotto with Leek Straw and Tomato Sauce

Vienna
Raspberry Omelette

Ingredients

Red Mullet

4 red mullet fillets,
each weighing approx. 70 g

Salt, freshly milled white pepper

lemon juice

1 tbsp oil

a little butter

Risotto

2 tbsp shallots, finely diced

2 tbsp olive oil

200 g risotto rice
(Vialone or Avorio)

salt, freshly milled white pepper

1 clove of garlic, peeled

2 sprigs of thyme

12,5 cl white wine, dry

500 ml hot chicken stock
(see glossary)

1 leek paste (see glossary)

Leek Straw

1/2 a leek,
tender green only

oil for deep-frying, salt

Tomato Sauce

1 l tomato stock (see glossary)

20-30 g cold butter

Potato Fritters

1 potato, as big as possible and firm when boiled, oil for deep-frying, salt

Peel the potato and cut lengthways into wafer-thin slices. Soak in luke-warm water for 15 minutes, then dry thoroughly on a cloth or in a small salad spinner. Deep-fry in 175°C to 180°C hot oil until golden-yellow, allow to drain on a piece of kitchen roll and salt very sparingly.

Stuffing

2 bunches of rucola, 2-3 tbsp balsamico dressing (see glossary), 150 g marinated salmon in thin slices, chive sauce (see glossary)

Clean and wash rucola and remove any coarse stalks, dry well, spin and briefly marinate in balsamico dressing. Layer three to four potato fritters with salmon and rucola in turn, as if making a lasagne, adding a little chive sauce to salmon and rucola in the process. Place on four plates, cover with potato fritters and serve immediately.

Preparation Hors d'œuvre

Preparation Main Course

Red Mullet and Risotto

To make the risotto, lightly braise the shallots in olive oil, stirring constantly until transparent, then add the rice and also braise until transparent, stirring almost continuously whilst seasoning with salt, pepper, the clove of garlic and the sprigs of thyme. Now add wine and allow to reduce. Stir rice frequently, adding hot chicken stock bit by bit until the liquid has boiled away. Stir the risotto as often as possible to prevent the rice from sticking to the bottom of the pan. Mix in the leek paste, spoon by spoon, at the very end. Whilst the risotto is cooking, allow the tomato stock (see glossary) to reduce by half to make the tomato sauce. Stir in the small, ice-cold pieces of butter just before serving in order to bind the stock somewhat. Briefly rinse red mullet fillets under cold water jet, dab thoroughly dry and season with salt, pepper and lemon juice. Heat oil in a frying pan, place red mullet fillets, skin down, into the pan and dot with a few small pieces of butter. Sear the fillets briefly, then finish cooking in the oven, pre-heated to 220°C, top heat, for 2 to 3 minutes.

Leek Straw

To make leek straw, cut leek into wafer-thin strips and deep-fry in 180°C hot oil for 20 to 30 seconds. The leek should be crispy but still green. Remove immediately, allow to drain on a piece of kitchen roll and salt sparingly.

Steigenberger Wine Recommendation

1995 Spätburgunder Rosé Sekt, medium-dry, Sektkellerei von Canal, Winningen, Germany

Vienna Raspberry Omelette

200 g curd cheese (20% fat), 3 egg yolks, zest of 1 lemon, 4 egg whites,
150 g sugar, 300 g raspberries, butter for frying, 2 tbsp cream, icing sugar for dusting

Pass the curd cheese through a sieve into a bowl, add egg yolks and stir thoroughly. Mix in lemon zest. Beat the egg whites with 70 g sugar to a creamy consistency using a rotary whisk. Mix the beaten egg whites carefully into the curd cheese mixture. Pre-heat the oven to 220°C. Mix 150 g of raspberries with the rest of the sugar in a glass bowl. Purée the remaining raspberries with a power mixer and then pass through a sieve. Heat some butter in two oven-proof, non-stick frying pans, approx. 18 cm in diameter. Using a ladle, put one quarter of the omelette mixture in each frying pan at a time, distributing evenly and smoothly. Allow omelettes to set lightly for around 2 minutes over medium heat, then place them for a further 8 minutes in the oven (center shelf). The volume now doubles. Remove the two omelettes. Sprinkle the raspberries over the omelettes using a spoon and fold each omelette in half.

Preparation Dessert

**Christine
Steigenberger**

Ingredients

Pea and Mint Soup
with Breton Lobster

Duck Legs
on Lentils

Goat's cheese
served slightly warm
with deep-fried Rucola
and Truffle Honey

Duck Legs

150 g Puy lentils

2 shallots, chopped

2 cloves of garlic, chopped

olive oil

2 tsp tomato purée

4 cl port

500 ml veal stock

500 ml vegetable stock

2 carrots, diced small

rosemary, thyme

pepper, salt

4 duck legs

2-4 slices of smoked bacon, diced

10 ml aceto balsamico

2 tsp cold butter

1 bunch of parsley, chopped

2 tomatoes, diced

Preparation Hors d'oeuvre

Pea and Mint Soup

500 g peas; 500 g mangetout, cut small; 5 shallots; 1 clove of garlic; 50 g icing sugar; 1 l vegetable stock; 750 ml cream; butter; olive oil; 3 sprigs of mint; 1 Breton lobster; vegetable broth

Peel shallots and garlic and briefly sweat in butter and olive oil. Put aside a few peas and mangetout before adding the remaining ones to the pot, dust with icing sugar and continue sweating. Pour in vegetable stock and add mint. Cook for 10 minutes and then purée the mixture through a sieve. Cook the lobster for 10 minutes in a hot vegetable broth. Remove and break open. Whip the cream. Arrange in soup plates the peas and mangetout that have been placed aside, ladle pea soup over them, dot with cream, top with lobster pieces and serve.

Preparation Main Course

Duck Legs on Lentils

Blanch lentils in salted water. Briefly sweat shallots, diced bacon and garlic in olive oil. Add tomato purée and allow to roast for a short time. Add drained lentils and pour in the port. Add the stock, carrots, thyme and rosemary and allow to simmer until lentils are al dente. Then season with salt and pepper, add aceto balsamico to taste and add the cold butter. Sear duck legs in olive oil, together with the garlic, rosemary and thyme. Continue to cook in the oven for approx. 30 minutes at 180°C. Place the lentils on the plates, top with a duck leg and garnish with parsley and tomato segments.

Steigenberger Wine Recommendation
2001 Bricco dell' Uccellone, Barbera d'Asti, Giacomo Bologna, Braida, Rocchetta Tanaro, Italy

Goat's Cheese served slightly warm

4 small goat's cheese, round; 1 bunch of rucola; 1 courgette; 4 toothpicks; truffle honey; olive oil

Cut courgette lengthways into wafer-thin strips. Wrap around goat's cheese and fix in place with the toothpicks. Lightly deep-fry the rucola in hot oil and allow to drain on a piece of kitchen roll. Briefly fry the goat's cheeses in olive oil in a pan, then bake in the oven for 10 minutes at 180°C. Arrange goat's cheese on the plates and top with truffle honey.

Preparation Dessert

**Claudia
Steigenberger**

Ingredients

Kid

1 prepared kid
with offal removed

2 onions, diced

2 carrots, diced

1-2 sticks of celery,
cleaned and roughly chopped

2-3 tbsp oil

1 clove of garlic

1 sprig of thyme

1 bay leaf

5-6 white peppercorns

2 juniper berries

salt, freshly milled white pepper

10 cl Noilly Prat

10 cl white wine, dry

hot water for topping up

lemon segments, lemon juice

flour for tossing

breadcrumbs for tossing

2 eggs

2 tbsp cream, whipped

oil for deep-frying

Potato Salad

600 g potatoes, firm boilers

2 shallots, diced

2 tsp hot mustard

2-3 tbsp wine vinegar

200 ml strong beef broth

salt, freshly milled white pepper

4-5 tbsp oil

1 bunch watercress

Asparagus
Solo

Baked Kid
on a warm Potato Salad

Panna cotta
with Strawberries
in Balsamico Caramel

Preparation Hors d'œuvre

Asparagus

20 asparagus spears, peeled; 1 bunch chives; 1 sprig of rosemary; 1 sprig of thyme; 50 g butter; 1 dash of white wine; sugar; salt; pepper; aluminium foil

Tie asparagus and chives into a bundle. Lay out aluminium foil. Place butter, rosemary, thyme and asparagus on foil. Add salt, pepper and a dash of white wine. Sprinkle sugar over. Now wrap the foil up tightly and cook in oven for approx. 20 minutes at 180°C. Serve on plate inside the foil so the full asparagus flavour can be enjoyed.

Preparation Main Course

Kid on Potato Salad

Cut up kid, with bones, into small pieces and run a cold water jet briefly over everything to remove any small bone fragments. Dab thoroughly dry and salt sparingly. Allow the prepared vegetables to glaze slightly in hot oil and season with garlic, thyme, the bay leaf, peppercorns, juniper berries, salt and pepper. Pour in Noilly Prat and white wine. Add kid portions and enough hot water to cover everything well. Bring to boil and then simmer at low heat for approx. 1 hour, until the meat is tender. Allow to cool in its own stock. In the meantime boil the potatoes. For the marinade, mix the mustard well with vinegar, beef broth, salt, pepper, shallots and oil. Cut the still warm potatoes into slices and place in the marinade, allowing them to cool and steep. Remove any unwanted leaves and all stalks from the watercress and wash it. Carefully fold under the potato salad just before serving.

Remove the kid portions from the stock and dab dry. Then rub with lemon segments, rub in lemon juice and season with salt and pepper. Take two soup plates, put flour in one and breadcrumbs in the other. Beat the eggs thoroughly in a third plate and add cream. Turn kid portions first in the flour, then in the egg-cream mix and then in the breadcrumbs. Press this coating lightly but firmly on and deep-fry the kid portions in a deep-fryer until golden-brown. Allow to drain well on a piece of kitchen roll and serve with the warm potato salad.

Steigenberger Wine Recommendation 2004 Münsterer Pittersberg, Silberkapsel, Kruger-Rumpf, Münster-Sarmsheim, Germany

Panna cotta

750 ml whipping cream, 1 orange, 1 lemon, 150 g sugar, 2 vanilla pods, 1/3 cinnamon stick, 1/4 star anise, 4 leaves of gelatine, Grand Marnier, Amaretto

Pour the cream into a pot. Press the juice from the orange and the lemon and add to the cream. Add the sugar and heat, without stirring, so the sugar does not burn to the bottom. Halve the vanilla pods, scrape out the pulp and add to the cream together with the cinnamon stick and the star anise. Bring briefly to the boil. Now soak the gelatine in cold water. Remove star anise and cinnamon stick from the cream. Whip the gelatine, the Grand Marnier, the Amaretto and the cream in a mixer. Pour into small moulds and stand in a cool place.

Aceto Balsamico Sauce

**300 g strawberries,
200 g sugar, 30 g butter,
750 ml orange juice,
4 tbsp old aceto balsamico**

Put sugar and butter in a frying pan over heat until the mixture forms a straw-coloured caramel. Pour in orange juice. Allow to simmer until the caramel has dissolved in the orange juice. Add aceto balsamico and continue simmering until the mix has the consistency of a syrup. Quarter the strawberries and put into the cooled syrup. Upturn the panna cotta onto plates and decorate with strawberries.

Preparation Dessert

Set amidst the vineyard-clad hills of the Pfalz region, right at the gates of the town of Deidesheim, this holiday hotel has been part of the Steigenberger Group since 1994. With its 124 rooms, the hotel is unusually furnished and equipped in the Anglo-American style of the 1930's to 1950's. Warm, strong colours, robust furniture, rough woven fabrics made from natural fibres, obligatory ceiling fans and the Wurlitzer jukebox in the bar all emphasise the hotel's casual, elegant flair.

Pfälzer Mozartkugeln (Black Pudding and Potato-Dough Dumplings)
on Creamed Sauerkraut and Truffled Mashed Potatoes

Ingredients

Mozartkugeln

150 g black pudding, without skin, diced

3 shallots

1 tbsp marjoram, freshly chopped

2 egg yolks

1 egg

30 g butter

300 g potatoes

2 tbsp flour

salt, pepper, nutmeg

Creamed Sauerkraut

40 g diced onions

20 g lard

250 g sauerkraut, pickled and marinated

1 bay leaf

2 juniper berries

1 clove

salt and pepper

3 tbsp dry Riesling

60 ml cream, whipped

sugar, marjoram

Truffled Mashed Potatoes

300 g potatoes

50 ml cream

50 ml milk

20 g butter

salt, pepper, nutmeg

1 tsp truffle oil (available from any well-stocked food shop)

Pfälzer Mozartkugeln (Black Pudding and Potato-Dough Dumplings)

Briefly sweat the shallots in 20 g butter, add the black pudding and brown. Season with marjoram and remove from heat. Mix in 10 g of butter and egg yolks. Allow the mixture to cool thoroughly. Once it starts to firm up, form 12 small balls. Press the boiled potatoes through a potato ricer and, adding flour, egg, salt, pepper and grated nutmeg, work into a smooth dough. Surround the black pudding balls with potato dough, form into dumplings and allow these to simmer gently in salted water for 20 minutes.

Creamed Sauerkraut

Lightly braise diced onion in lard. Wash the sauerkraut in cold water and add to the onions, then add white wine. Season to taste with salt, pepper, juniper berries, cloves and a pinch of sugar. Allow to simmer for 20 minutes. Now remove the juniper berries and the bay leaf and carefully fold under the whipped cream.

Preparation

Truffled Mashed Potatoes

Heat cream, milk and butter in a pot. Boil the potatoes in salted water for approx. 18 minutes, drain and press through a potato ricer. Gradually add the heated milk/cream to the potato mix, beat well with a whisk and then season to taste with salt, pepper, grated nutmeg and truffle oil.

Steigenberger Wine Recommendation 2003 Forster Ungeheuer, Riesling Spätlese dry, Reichsrat von Buhl, Deidesheim, Germany

Steigenberger Duisburger Hof has enjoyed a reputation for special excellence since 1927. Spacious, elegant conference rooms and tastefully furnished hotel rooms, high-class cuisine and fine wines await the guest.
Located opposite the Deutsche Oper on the banks of the river Rhine, the hotel is ideally situated for those wishing to get to know the modern Ruhr region and experience the major structural and cultural changes it has undergone.

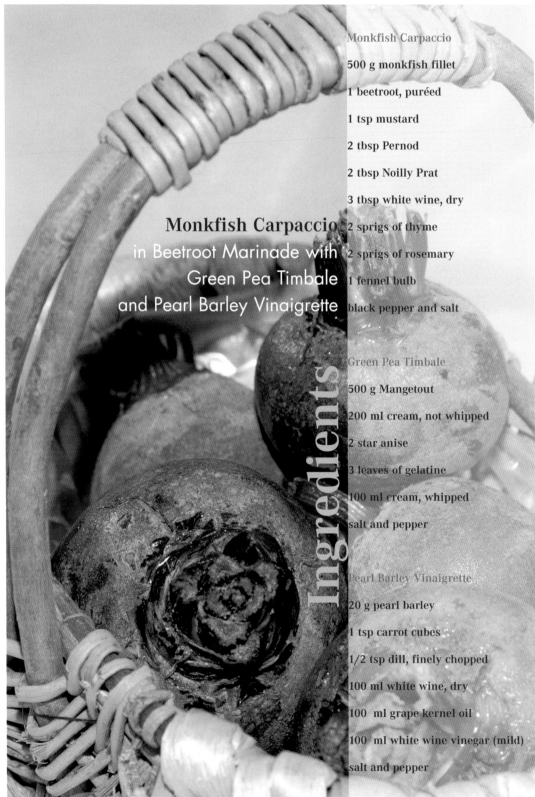

Monkfish Carpaccio
in Beetroot Marinade with Green Pea Timbale and Pearl Barley Vinaigrette

Ingredients

Monkfish Carpaccio

500 g monkfish fillet

1 beetroot, puréed

1 tsp mustard

2 tbsp Pernod

2 tbsp Noilly Prat

3 tbsp white wine, dry

2 sprigs of thyme

2 sprigs of rosemary

1 fennel bulb

black pepper and salt

Green Pea Timbale

500 g Mangetout

200 ml cream, not whipped

2 star anise

3 leaves of gelatine

100 ml cream, whipped

salt and pepper

Pearl Barley Vinaigrette

20 g pearl barley

1 tsp carrot cubes

1/2 tsp dill, finely chopped

100 ml white wine, dry

100 ml grape kernel oil

100 ml white wine vinegar (mild)

salt and pepper

Monkfish Carpaccio in Beetroot Marinade

Mix all ingredients to make the marinade. Then season the fish with salt and pepper, turn in the marinade and briefly allow to steep. Now wrap the fish in clingfilm and freeze for 6 hours. This allows the fish to be cut thinly on a cutter.

Preparation

Green Pea Timbale

Boil the mangetout with the cream and the star anise until soft, then purée and pass through a sieve. Soak the gelatine, dissolve and then mix under the pea mixture, season. Fold in the whipped cream and fill four moulds with the mixture.

Pearl Barley Vinaigrette

Mix all ingredients to make a vinaigrette.

Steigenberger Wine Recommendation 2004 White Burgundy, Silberkapsel, Kruger-Rumpf, Münster-Sarmsheim, Nahe, Germany

Steigenberger Frankfurter Hof in Frankfurt/Main welcomes the guest with all the flair of an international grand hotel. Located right at the heart of the banking and financial metropolis, this luxury hotel looks back on more than one hundred years of excellence. Such tradition is appreciated by visitors from all corners of the world. 332 elegant rooms and suites, 18 conference rooms accommodating up to 450 people, plus modern spa facilities, provide a luxurious ambience to meet the most sophisticated tastes. The gastronomic array is also an attraction. Between them, the gourmet restaurant Français, the Japanese speciality restaurant Iroha, Oscar's Bistro and the Hofgarten restaurant cater for every culinary desire.

Frankfurt Green Sauce served in a Glass with Crostini and Steak Tartare

Ingredients

Green Sauce

400 g crème fraîche

1 portion herbs
for Frankfurt Green Sauce
(see glossary)

100 g horseradish, hot

salt and pepper

5 leaves of gelatine

herbs for garnishing

Crostini

1/2 baguette

olive oil

Tartar

100 g steak tartare

1 anchovy

5 capers

1 shallot, diced

a little mustard

salt, pepper

Green Sauce

Soak gelatine in water and then dissolve in a little crème fraîche. Add this to the remaining crème fraîche, add the horseradish and stir, season to taste with salt and pepper. Divide the mixture, fill one half into four glasses and stand in a cool place. Finely purée the other half with the Frankfurt herbs. Now top the white mixture in the glasses with the green mixture. Place filled glasses once more in a cold place. Garnish with fresh herbs.

Crostini

Cut the baguette crossways into slices (long enough to protrude over the top of the glass) and roast in hot olive oil until golden.

Tartar

Mix steak tartar with all finely chopped ingredients and season to taste.

How to serve: Place crostini over the top of the glass and top with a „nut" of steak tartar. Place glass on a side plate and serve.

Preparation

Steigenberger Wine Recommendation

2004 Von Buhl Riesling Spätlese dry, Reichsrat von Buhl, Deidesheim, Germany

Steigenberger Conti Hansa is located right in the centre of the port city of Kiel, directly opposite the Firth of Kiel. Visit the "Kiel Week" event or the annual music festival or simply watch the comings and goings in the harbour – the elegance and high-end ambience of the hotel provides the right setting, and it is ideally situated for setting out on local excursions. Nine conference rooms also await the business guest at Steigenberger Conti Hansa.

Shrimp Soup

Ingredients

2 onions

1 leek

2 carrots

50 g butter

60 g flour

750 ml fish stock (see glossary)

250 ml cream

80 g shrimp soup paste

100 g North Sea shrimps

dill

olive oil

Preparation

Clean and dice onions, carrots and leek. Add olive oil to a pot, sweat the vegetables and dust with flour.

Continue to sweat a little longer. Now add fish stock and cream and stir well. Pass soup through a sieve.

Add shrimp soup paste and season to taste with salt and pepper. Add North Sea shrimps and garnish with dill.

Steigenberger Wine Recommendation 2003 Welschriesling, Weingut Nehrer, Burgenland, Austria

Above the beautiful Austrian town of Krems, surrounded by fine old vines and blessed with a splendid view over the Danube valley, Steigenberger Avance Hotel is a true country home amidst the vineyards. Set on Goldberg hill, the hotel provides first-class comfort as well as appealing wellness and relaxation options. Explore the picturesque Wachau region or enjoy a wide range of sports and recreation facilities. The hotel also features an oasis of wellness as well as a therapy centre.

Cream of Beetroot Soup
with Butter Dumplings

Ingredients

Creamed Soup

2 kg beetroot

300 g onions

2 tsp caraway seeds

olive oil

approx. 1 l vegetable consommé

500 ml whipping cream

salt

freshly milled white pepper

Butter Dumplings

50 g butter

2 egg yolks

100 g flour

2 egg whites

25 g horseradish

chervil

Creamed Soup

Peel beetroot, cut into rough cubes and, together with the roughly chopped onions, sear briefly in olive oil. Add vegetable consommé, season and allow to simmer until the beetroot is soft. Add whipping cream, purée, then pass through a fine sieve and season well.

Preparation

Butter Dumplings

Beat butter and egg yolks until fluffy. Carefully fold under the mixture the flour, beaten egg whites and horseradish.

Cut four large or several small dumplings from the mixture, put into slightly salted water and simmer or poach carefully.

Remove dumplings with care and immediately put in ice water. This will ensure they stay firm and retain their nice shape.

Before serving, blend soup again using a power mixer in order to generate an airy foam. Pour equal amounts into soup plates, place the warm butter dumplings in the centre and garnish with chervil.

Steigenberger Beverage Recommendation Staatl. Fachingen Medium

Steigenberger Mannheimer Hof is located right next to the city of Mannheim's most famous landmark, the Water Tower. Opposite is the Mannheim Congress Center, and even the "chessboard" city's main shop and stroll area, the "Planken", is only five minutes walk away. The four-star hotel's charming garden restaurant serves summery dishes and the Avalon restaurant offers international cuisine. The "Schatzkistl", in the hotel basement, is a cosy, much frequented cabaret venue with a constantly changing show.

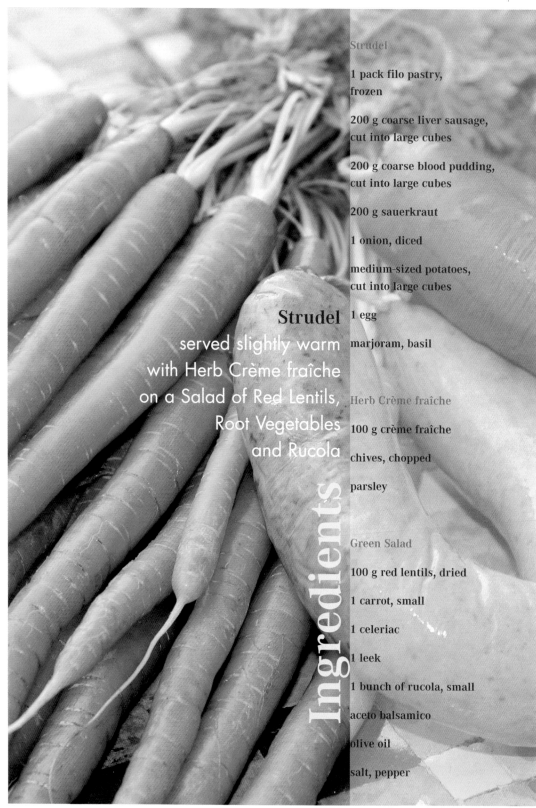

Strudel
served slightly warm
with Herb Crème fraîche
on a Salad of Red Lentils,
Root Vegetables
and Rucola

Ingredients

Strudel

1 pack filo pastry, frozen

200 g coarse liver sausage, cut into large cubes

200 g coarse blood pudding, cut into large cubes

200 g sauerkraut

1 onion, diced

medium-sized potatoes, cut into large cubes

1 egg

marjoram, basil

Herb Crème fraîche

100 g crème fraîche

chives, chopped

parsley

Green Salad

100 g red lentils, dried

1 carrot, small

1 celeriac

1 leek

1 bunch of rucola, small

aceto balsamico

olive oil

salt, pepper

Boil the potatoes in salted water until soft. Sweat onions in hot oil, add potatoes and fry until both vegetables have a little colour. Now add sauerkraut, the black puddding and liver sausage. Season with salt, pepper, marjoram and basil, remove from heat and allow to cool.

Place filo pastry on a lightly floured surface and allow to defrost. The pastry should measure approx. 40 x 20 cm. Now spread the cool filling over the pastry dough, leaving approx. 2 to 3 cm free around the edges. Brush the edges with some of the beaten egg. Carefully roll up the strudel, press the ends together and fold under. Now brush the entire strudel with the remaining beaten egg and bake in the oven for approx. 25 to 30 minutes, using the fan. Once baked, allow the

Preparation

strudel to cool completely. This makes it easier to cut. Cook red lentils in slightly salted water until soft. Finely dice carrot, leek and celeriac (lentil size) and also boil until soft. Once the lentils and the vegetables are cool, marinate everything in aceto balsamico, olive oil, salt and pepper. Now season the crème fraîche to taste with parsley, chives and salt and pepper. Wash rucola and drain well. Cut strudel into eight equal sections and re-heat briefly in the oven. Now put rucola on four plates, top with lentil salad (keeping the centre free), and place the strudel sections in the centre, with one or two dabs of herb crème fraîche next to them. Garnish with three perfect basil leaves.

Steigenberger Wine Recommendation 2004 Dornfelder Qualitätswein dry, Weingut Dr. Bürklin-Wolf, Pfalz, Germany

Steigenberger SPA Hotel Norderney will be opening on the East Frisian island of Norderney in 2008. This new resort hotel will be integrated into the historic "Conversationshaus", which has been the island's spa since the early 19th century, a meeting place for the rich and famous from both home and abroad. The building is now being renovated, in all its former glory, and extended with a hotel complex consisting of interior courtyard, wellness and spa facilities as well as quality gastronomic venues. Situated around 250 metres from the beach, right in the centre of town, Steigenberger SPA Hotel Norderney will provide a rich variety of services to guests seeking a holiday, leisure pursuits, wellness or conference facilities.

Trio of Aromas

Ingredients

4 small tomatoes

220 g mozzarella

basil

aceto balsamico

200 g minced beef

2 spring onions

1 egg

2 sprigs flat-leaved parsley

200 ml chive sauce (see glossary)

1 tin sturgeon caviar (approx. 40 g)

pepper, salt, cayenne pepper

4 round slices of pumpernickel

200 g North Sea shrimps

1 small apple

400 ml chive sauce (see glossary)

1 bunch spring onions

100 ml chicken broth

salt, pepper

1 small glass of pickled gherkins

chives, chopped

Cut a thin slice from bottom of tomatoes so they can stand well. Now halve crossways. Using a small cutter with a slightly greater diameter than the tomatoes, cut out rounds from mozzarella slices, place basil and mozzarella rounds on bottom halves of tomatoes and top with the other halves, the flowering ones. Sprinkle aceto balsamico all round.

Cut spring onions into small strips and blanch. Chop parsley small. Mix both with the egg yolk and the minced beef to make a tartar, season to taste with salt, pepper and cayenne pepper. Shape tartar into a small tower and place on the pumpernickel slices. Top with spoonful of chive sauce and decorate with the caviar.

Preparation

Wash North Sea shrimps, drain and place in a bowl. Core and dice the apple. Cut spring onions into small rounds and blanch. Chop pickled gherkins small. Now add everything to the North Sea shrimps and mix well. Add the chive sauce and season to taste with a little chicken broth and spices. To finish off, gently fold finely cut chives under the mixture.

Steigenberger Wine Recommendation

2002 Forster Pechstein Riesling Spätlese dry, Reichsrat von Buhl, Deidesheim, Germany

Steigenberger Strandhotel Zingst
will be opening in the idyllic
Baltic Sea spa resort of Zingst in
2006. With an impressive range of
wellness and leisure facilities,
charming classic spa architecture,
a remarkable interior plus a range
of high-quality services, Steigenberger Strandhotel Zingst will be
a very special destination on the
Fischland-Darß peninsula in the
province of Mecklenburg Pomera-
nia. Situated directly on the main
promenade, pier and beach, this
four-star hotel will offer discerning guests a choice of 104 double
rooms and 17 suites, as well as
an inviting gastronomic area in
restaurant and bar.

Matjes Herring Salad

Ingredients

500 g matjes herring fillsets

1 apple

4 tbsp cream

4 tbsp crème fraîche

6 pickled gherkins

gherkin juice

4 spring onions

1 bunch chives

oil, vegetable broth

pepper, salt, lemon juice

100 ml orange juice

Preparation

Chop spring onions and blanch. Quench in ice water. Stir together oil, vegetable broth, cream, crème fraîche and lemon juice. Season with salt and pepper. Core, peel and dice the apple, finely dice gherkins, add to mix and stir in. Clean the matjes herrings, cut into small pieces and add to cream sauce. Sprinkle with chives and allow to steep for approx. 24 hours in the refrigerator. Season to taste with orange juice and gherkin juice.

Steigenberger Wine Recommendation 2004 Sauvignon Blanc, Weingut Nehrer, Burgenland, Austria

Steigenberger Hotel Bellerive au Lac is located on Lake Zurich promenade, close to the opera house and financial and business district. In lovingly restoring and renovating this historic monument, architect Tilla Theus has succeeded in uniting the distinguished history of the Bellerive with the comfort standards of a modern business hotel.

This small yet elegant inner-city hotel combines modern lifestyle with the cool charm of the City of Zurich and is pleased to welcome lovers of culture and business travellers alike.

Veal's Head Cheeks
braised in Oil
with Aceto Lentils

Ingredients

Veal's Head Cheeks

320 g veal's head cheeks

4 sprigs of rosemary,
stalks removed and chopped

4 sprigs of thyme,
stalks removed and chopped

4 cloves of garlic

400 ml olive oil

Lentil Salad

160 g brown lentils

160 g shallots, diced

4 bay leaves

4 sprigs of rosemary,
stalks removed and chopped

4 sprigs of thyme,
stalks removed and chopped

40 ml olive oil

salt, freshly milled white pepper

instant beef bouillon

aceto balsamico

Vinaigrette

40 ml sunflower oil

40 ml olive oil

40 ml aromatic vinegar

120 g shallots, finely chopped

3 tsp chives, chopped

1 tsp sugar

8 green salad leaves for garnishing

Lentil Salad

Soak lentils in cold water. Then season with bay leaves, some salt and freshly milled pepper. Boil until soft but still firm in a little beef bouillon, rosemary, thyme and 4 tbsp. of aceto balsamico, then strain and briefly rinse. Heat olive oil and add shallots. Toss lentils in this and season with salt and freshly milled pepper. Put in a bowl. Now add vinaigrette and serve with a green salad.

Vinaigrette

Mix aromatic vinegar, olive oil, sunflower oil, chopped shallots, salt, freshly milled pepper and, if preferred, a little sugar. Add the chopped chives at the end and season to taste once more.

Preparation

Veal's Head Cheeks

Allow veal's head cheeks to marinate for at least 72 hours in a mixture of two sprigs each of chopped rosemary and thyme, stalks removed, garlic and some olive oil. Remove cheeks from marinade and season with salt and pepper. Lightly brown in a frying pan, then place in an oven dish. Add the garlic and two sprigs each of rosemary and thyme. Pour in olive oil to barely cover the cheeks and braise in the oven, covered, at 150°C for 45 minutes.

Steigenberger Wine Recommendation
2002 Chanteauvieux Dôle du Valais, Wallis, Switzerland

Elegance and hospitality are long established at this hotel. Steigenberger Europäischer Hof has been a feature of the townscape of Baden-Baden for more than 165 years. Facing the Kurhaus with its world-renowned casino and the beautiful theatre, this building, rich in tradition, radiates the allure of the Belle Époque. Today, too, the guest is treated like royalty, be it unwinding in the wellness complex Europe Spa, using the broad range of conference and seminar facilities or trying the delicacies of the hotel cuisine.

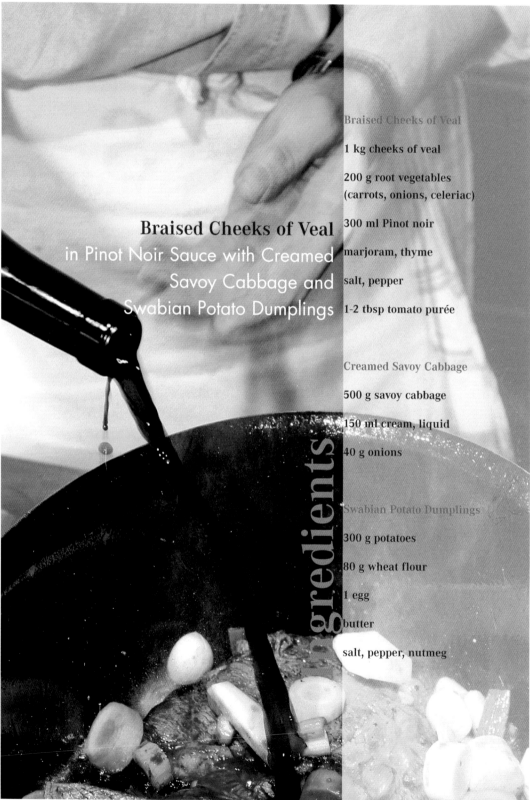

Braised Cheeks of Veal
in Pinot Noir Sauce with Creamed Savoy Cabbage and Swabian Potato Dumplings

Ingredients

Braised Cheeks of Veal

1 kg cheeks of veal

200 g root vegetables (carrots, onions, celeriac)

300 ml Pinot noir

marjoram, thyme

salt, pepper

1-2 tbsp tomato purée

Creamed Savoy Cabbage

500 g savoy cabbage

150 ml cream, liquid

40 g onions

Swabian Potato Dumplings

300 g potatoes

80 g wheat flour

1 egg

butter

salt, pepper, nutmeg

Cheeks of Veal

Roughly remove any surplus fat from the veal cheeks and sear in a roasting pan. Add diced root vegetables and roast. As soon as the vegetables have a good strong colour, add one to two tablespoons of tomato purée. Continue to roast and pour in the Pinot noir. Allow the wine to reduce until everything in the pan begins to roast again, then add more wine. Repeat this process three times, taking care to stir constantly so that the browned residue does not burn. Now cover meat with water, add herbs and braise until tender for approx. 40 minutes with the lid on. Remove the meat from the pan and strain the remaining herb residue through a fine sieve. Season with salt and pepper and allow to reduce to one third. The sauce can be thickened further if desired, either by reducing (this increases the flavour intensity of the sauce) or by adding food starch.

Preparation

Steigenberger Wine Recommendation

2001 Oberbergener Baßgeige, Spätburgunder, Qualitätswein dry, Weingut Schwarzer Adler, Franz Keller, Baden, Germany

Creamed Savoy Cabbage

Remove the stalk of the savoy cabbage, peel onions and cut both into fine strips. Put the onions in a hot frying pan and sweat until transparent, then add cut cabbage and continue to braise. Add liquid cream to the cabbage and onion mix and simmer until soft. Season with salt and pepper to taste.

Swabian Potato Dumplings

Peel potatoes and boil in salted water until soft, drain and allow steam to evaporate and then press through a potato ricer. It is also possible to use a potato masher but care has to be taken that no lumps are left. Knead riced potato with egg and flour until homogenous and season with salt and pepper. Form short, finger-thick rolls ("Schupfnudeln") and boil in salted water. Then toss in melted butter until they take on a slightly brown colour.

Located in a prime site in this historical town, the Steigenberger Hotel Bad Homburg is the epitome of magnificent hotel tradition. Not far from the metropolis of Frankfurt, in the hills of the Taunus, visitors can enjoy tranquillity amidst stylish art déco surroundings. This 169-room hotel particularly attracts business travellers who appreciate extensive conference facilities in a quiet location.

Corn-fed Chicken Breast stuffed with Morels
on Tarragon Sauce with glazed Spring Vegetables and diced Potatoes in a Nest

Ingredients

Corn-fed Chicken Breast

4 corn-fed chicken breasts with skin

10 g dried morels, soaked and washed well

2 tbsp shallots, diced

1 tbsp butter

4 cl sherry or light-coloured port

1 egg white and a little cream

Spring Vegetables

4 portions vegetables (young carrots, spring onions, mangetout etc.)

3-4 tbsp butter and some sugar for glazing

salt and pepper

5-6 very large potatoes

oil for deep-frying

2 tea strainers for moulding the nests

Tarragon Sauce

600 ml vegetable stock

50 ml white wine

150 ml cream

a few sprigs of tarragon

1-2 tbsp flour-butter thickener (see glossary)

Corn-fed Chicken Breast

Briefly rinse chicken breasts and dab dry with a piece of kitchen roll, removing any left-over feathers. Remove the inner fillets, cut small and put into freezer for a short while. Squeeze any remaining water from the morels and chop finely. Strain through a cloth the water in which the morels were soaked. Briefly sweat the chopped morels together with the diced shallots in a little butter until they start to show some colour. Add the sherry, season the morels with salt and pepper and put in a cool place. Put the chicken fillets together with the egg white and the cream in a moulinette to make a farce. Stir in the cooled morels, season the farce and scoop it into a piping bag. Cut a pocket in the chicken breasts using a small knife and stuff with the farce (or stuff the farce beneath the chicken skin). Brown the chicken breasts in oil and cook on a grill in the oven at 220°C for approx. 10 to 12 minutes.

Preparation

Spring Vegetables

Blanch (see glossary) the vegetables and then briefly fry in butter in a frying pan. Glaze with sugar. Peel some of the potatoes, grate finely and season with pepper and salt. Use a tea strainer to mould a little nest and deep-fry in hot oil. Allow to cool and put the nests aside. Now peel the remaining potatoes, dice small and deep-fry. Finally spoon into the nests.

Tarragon Sauce

Add a dash of port to the pan with the chicken residues and then add approx. 600 ml chicken stock and simmer slowly to reduce. Add tarragon and the water in which the morels soaked and reduce again. Add a little butter to make a sauce and season with pepper and salt.

Steigenberger Wine Recommendation 2002 Iphöfer Kalb, Silvaner Qualitätswein dry, Weingut Hans Wirsching, Franken, Germany

Austrian Empress Elisabeth was quick to appreciate the health benefits of Franconian spa town Bad Kissingen. Well-tended parks invite quiet strolls, and history-lovers can discover everywhere the traces of famous royal and imperial guests. Steigenberger Kurhaus Hotel is an exclusive setting in which to relax in luxury. The hotel's own pool and fitness club caters for the well-being of the guest, as do the Beauty Farm and the Thalasso Therapy and Health Centre.

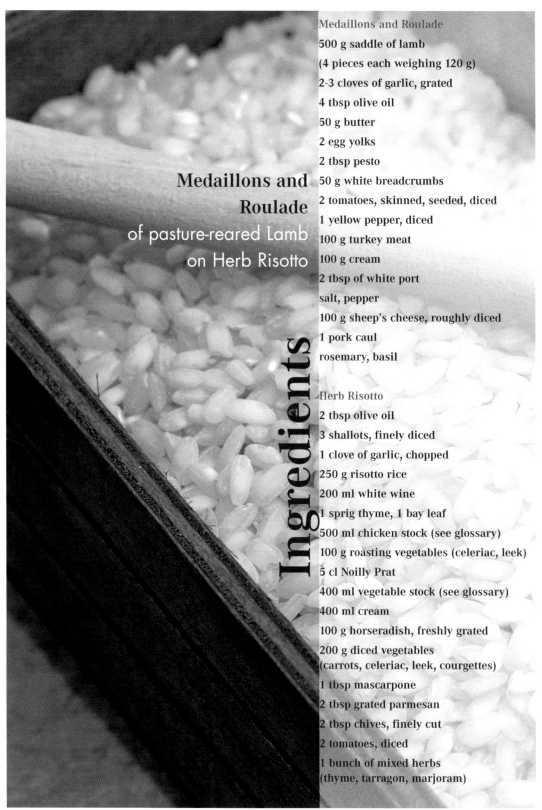

Medaillons and Roulade
of pasture-reared Lamb on Herb Risotto

Ingredients

Medaillons and Roulade

500 g saddle of lamb
(4 pieces each weighing 120 g)

2-3 cloves of garlic, grated

4 tbsp olive oil

50 g butter

2 egg yolks

2 tbsp pesto

50 g white breadcrumbs

2 tomatoes, skinned, seeded, diced

1 yellow pepper, diced

100 g turkey meat

100 g cream

2 tbsp of white port

salt, pepper

100 g sheep's cheese, roughly diced

1 pork caul

rosemary, basil

Herb Risotto

2 tbsp olive oil

3 shallots, finely diced

1 clove of garlic, chopped

250 g risotto rice

200 ml white wine

1 sprig thyme, 1 bay leaf

500 ml chicken stock (see glossary)

100 g roasting vegetables (celeriac, leek)

5 cl Noilly Prat

400 ml vegetable stock (see glossary)

400 ml cream

100 g horseradish, freshly grated

200 g diced vegetables
(carrots, celeriac, leek, courgettes)

1 tbsp mascarpone

2 tbsp grated parmesan

2 tbsp chives, finely cut

2 tomatoes, diced

1 bunch of mixed herbs
(thyme, tarragon, marjoram)

Medaillons and Roulade

Cut four medaillons, each weighing 60 g, from two saddles of lamb, season, marinate with some garlic and briefly fry on both sides. Beat butter and egg yolks until fluffy, mix with pesto and white breadcrumbs, season to taste, portion onto medaillons and put in a cool place.

Now season the remaining two saddles of lamb, marinate, fry briefly and put in a cool place. Briefly sweat tomatoes and the yellow pepper in olive oil. Put the turkey meat, the cream and the white port in a mixer to make a fine farce, season to taste with salt, pepper and some garlic. Mix the sheep's cheese, the chopped herbs and the diced pepper and tomato into the farce.

Spread out the wet pork caul and cover with approx. 1/2 cm of farce (approx. the size of the saddle of lamb). Place one lamb saddle onto the farce on the caul and spread some farce over it. Then top with the second saddle of lamb and spread some farce over it. Close the caul over everything in such a way that the two lamb saddles lie one on top of the other. Roast the roulade for approx. 15 minutes, and the medaillons for approx. 5 minutes, in the oven at 160°C until the meat is pink.

Herb Risotto

Lightly braise the shallots and the garlic over low heat in olive oil, add risotto rice and braise for 2 to 3 minutes, then pour in 150 ml white wine and add the herbs. Add the chicken stock little by little and cook the rice until al dente, stirring constantly. Allow to cool.

Braise the roasting vegetables in butter until translucent, then add the remaining white wine and the Noilly Prat. Pour in chicken stock and reduce by half. Season with salt and pepper. Boil the diced vegetables in salted water until cooked. Bring the cooled risotto briefly to the boil with the cooked diced vegetables and season to taste with salt, pepper and chives. Gently fold cream, horseradish, mascarpone and herbs under the risotto. Add grated parmesan to taste and garnish with diced tomato.

Steigenberger Wine Recommendation 2002 Zweigelt Hochberg, Weingut Nehrer, Burgenland, Austria

Next door to the magnificent Spa Lower Saxony Spa Park, Steigenberger Hotel Bad Pyrmont is an oasis of relaxation and tranquillity. This luxurious hotel has been providing an exclusive ambience since 1993. An oriental-styled wellness centre with swimming pool, sauna, steam bath, whirlpools and fitness room promotes the guest's well-being, as do the medical facilities and the hotel's own beauty salon, Pyrmontana.

Fried Turbot and Scallops
on Pumpkin and Ginger Sauce with Rice

Ingredients

Turbot and Scallops

500 g turbot fillet

350 g scallops, freshly scooped from shells

400 ml fish stock (see glossary)

3 tbsp olive oil

100 g butter

salt, pepper, coriander powder

Pumpkin and Ginger Sauce

500 g fresh pumpkin or 250 g pumpkin flesh

1 root of fresh ginger, cut into fine stripes or grated

250 ml white wine

400 ml white port

250 ml cream

2 shallots

200 ml vegetable stock

salt, pepper, sugar

3 tbsp pumpkinseed oil

4 portions rice

Pumpkin and Ginger Sauce

Seed the pumpkin, scoop out the flesh and chop small. Lightly sweat the shallots in some pumpkinseed oil, add sugar and the pumpkin flesh and allow to caramelise a little. Add fresh ginger and allow to boil with white wine, port, vegetable stock and cream. Purée finely in a mixer or with a power mixer and then pass through a fine sieve. Boil rice and serve with a little of the pumpkin purée.

Preparation

Turbot and Scallops

Sear turbot and scallops for approx. 4 minutes in a non-stick frying pan with 3 tbsp of olive oil or butter over medium to strong heat, so no juice escapes and they become nice and golden. Remove turbot and scallops and keep warm whilst adding fish stock to the pan residues.

Season with coriander and then serve with all other ingredients.

Steigenberger Wine Recommendation

2004 Winninger Uhlen, Riesling Spätlese dry,
Freiherr von Heddesdorff, Winningen, Mosel, Germany

Steigenberger Hotel Berlin is just
a stone's throw from Kurfürsten-
damm, the city's famous shop-
and-stroll boulevard. Luxurious
rooms and suites, a genteel atmosphere and excellent service make
a stay something special. A business centre is open 24 hours a
day and, as for matters culinary,
Holger Zurbrüggen serves Italian-
Japanese cuisine in gourmet
restaurant Louis. The banqueting
facilities, with ballroom, and the
14 conference rooms make Steigenberger Hotel Berlin the ideal
venue for any event.

Loup de mer
in Dashi and Saffron Stock

Ingredients

600 g sea bass
(Loup de mer)

1 tsp saffron

2 tsp dashi
(dried bonito,
available from Asian shops)

4 cl Noilly Prat

200 ml fish stock (see glossary)
or water

1/2 courgette

2 mini-peppers

4 caper berries

120 g couscous

4 spring onions

2 dried tomatoes

4 cherry tomatoes

4 spears of green asparagus

1 tbsp tempura flour

40 ml olive oil

1 lemon

salt

Mix saffron, dashi, Noilly Prat and fish stock and bring to boil in a pot. Put the couscous in a sieve on the pot and steam for 8 minutes. Then pour the stock over twice.

Preparation

Blanch the vegetables in the remaining stock and bind with the tempura flour (see glossary).

Clean the fish fillets, sprinkle with lemon juice and salt them. Sear the fish, skin side down, turn and allow to steep slowly.

Steigenberger Wine Recommendation

2004 Grauer Burgunder, Silberkapsel, Kruger-Rumpf, Münster-Sarmsheim, Nahe, Germany

62

Parkhotel Dresden-Radebeul with its impressive architectural flair is located at the foot of the Lössnitz vineyards. The main building and the "Villa Park" both retain their Italian style. From the foyer to the individual room, the guest is accompanied by modern art masterpieces from some of the greatest artists of our time. The 1,000 m² large wellness area and the hotel's own "Bionouvelle" beauty salon, are equally impressive, offering the opportunity to relax and spend pleasant hours indulging body, mind and soul.

Stuffed Haunch of Rabbit
in Buttermilk Sauce with Beetroot and Potato Dumplings

Ingredients

4 rabbit haunches, medium-sized

750 ml buttermilk for marinating

2 bunches of root vegetables

4 pieces of pork caul, approx. 20 x 20 cm

200 g black pudding

100 g onions

butter

some oil

1 tsp tomato purée

250 ml game stock (see glossary)

250 ml buttermilk

1 glass beetroot balls (drained weight 520g)

1/2 bunch of spring onions

600 g potatoes, boiled

200 g flour

2 eggs

2 slices of white bread

some potato starch

salt, pepper, nutmeg, marjoram

fresh herbs for garnishing

Remove bones from rabbit haunches. Marinate the meat together with a bunch of root vegetables for two to three days in a buttermilk marinade spiced with salt and pepper. For the farce, finely dice black pudding and onions. Heat a little butter and briefly sweat the diced onion in it until transparent. Add the diced black pudding and allow to melt at low heat. If necessary, season with salt and pepper and some fresh marjoram. Allow to cool.

Carefully remove the rabbit haunches from the buttermilk marinade, dab dry with kitchen roll and place on the pieces of pork caul. Now stuff the rabbit haunches with the black pudding farce and roll firmly, but carefully, in the pork caul. Brown the stuffed rabbit haunches on all sides in some oil. Add fresh root vegetables and tomato purée to the pan residues and reduce. Pour in a little gravy two or three times and allow to

Preparation

reduce. Then fill up with buttermilk marinade and braise in the oven (in own juices) for approx. 30 minutes. In the meantime prepare the potato dumplings. Press the boiled potatoes through a potato ricer, stir in flour and eggs and season with salt and a pinch of grated nutmeg. Cut off the rind of the sliced bread, cut into cubes and roast these in a frying pan in a little fat. Form three small dumplings per person, approx. 60 g each in weight, putting three to four of the bread cubes in the middle of each dumpling. Turn the dumplings in potato starch (this gives them a nice glossy appearance and a smooth surface). Put the dumplings into boiling salted water and simmer for approx. 12 minutes. Allow the beetroot balls to glaze over low heat in a little butter. Wash the spring onions and cut into 8 to 10 cm lengths. Sweat in butter and season with salt and pepper. Remove the cooked rabbit haunches from the gravy, strain the gravy, reduce and bind with a sauce binder, if necessary. Season to taste with salt and pepper and finish with butter flakes. Cut the rabbit haunches crossways and serve on pre-warmed plates, with the stuffing showing. Pour a little gravy over meat and plate. Place the potato dumplings topped with breadcrumb-butter (see glossary) all around the haunches and intersperse with beetroot balls and glazed spring onions. Sprinkle with freshly chopped herbs.

Steigenberger Wine Recommendation Veuve Clicquot brut

For a long time now Duesseldorf has enjoyed an international reputation as a cultural and fashion metropolis. Steigenberger Parkhotel, situated at the beginning of the famous "Königsallee", right in the centre of North Rhine-Westphalia's capital, offers refined hospitality in a magnificent metropolitan setting. With the Hofgarten and Deutsche Oper am Rhein right next door, this hotel, rich in tradition, is an much-loved meeting place for guests from all over the world.

Breast of Quail in Champignon
on Creamed Savoy Cabbage with Red Wine Sauce

Ingredients

6 extra-large champignons

1 whole quail

1 chicken breast fillet

200 ml cream

1 small savoy cabbage

250 g butter

salt, pepper, nutmeg

red wine sauce (see glossary)

2 egg whites

Cut the quail breasts away from the upper centre bone and remove the skin. Remove the stalks from four champignons and carefully scoop out using a small spoon (they must not break). Dice the chicken breast fillets, chop up finely in a food processor, add two egg whites and season with salt and pepper. Then add the cream, little by little, until a fluffy mixture (farce) is created. Spread a little farce around the inside of the scooped-out champignons, season the quail breast halves, place in the champignons and press until there is no gap. Now cover thickly with the farce until the quail breast halves are completely covered.

Remove the stalks of the two remaining champignons. Trim the tops in such a way that they make lids for the four stuffed champignons. Season the topped champignons from above and brush with melted butter. Briefly boil savoy cabbage leaves in boiling water, dry well and cut into fine stripes. Now melt butter briefly (not allowing it to gain any colour), pour in some cream and allow to simmer. Season with salt, pepper and grated nutmeg. Bake the stuffed champignons in the oven at 160 to 170°C for approx. 12 to 14 minutes. Then allow to stand for a good 1 to 2 minutes and halve lengthways. Place some savoy cabbage in the center of the pre-warmed plates and top each with two halves of champignons. Heat up red wine sauce and trickle over the champignons.

Preparation

Steigenberger Wine Recommendation
2003 Cuvée Belleruche,
M. Chapoutier, Côtes du Rhône, France

Attractively located on an Alster river canal, right in the city centre, Steigenberger Hotel Hamburg features 226 luxurious rooms and suites as well as extensive facilities for conferences and business meetings. In this typical Hanseatic brick building, priority is also given to culinary treats. Gourmet restaurant Calla spoils its gourmets with featuring eurasian specialities rich in unusual flavours and combinations. In summer, the large terrace invites to linger. Steigenberger Hotel Hamburg makes the guest feel truly comfortable.

Roast Saddle of Venison
with Hoisin Sauce, Apple-Celeriac Purée and Cep Mushrooms

Ingredients

Roast Saddle of Venison

1 kg saddle of venison

1 tbsp mixed spices
(star anise, bay leaf, coriander, juniper berries, cloves, whole allspice, black pepper)

125 ml game stock (see glossary)

100 ml red port

3 tsp hoisin sauce

30 g cold, diced butter

Apple-Celeriac Purée

500 g celeriac

200 g potatoes

240 g apples (Cox Orange Pippin)

1 tbsp brown butter

1 tbsp crème fraîche

Cep Mushrooms

250-300 g cep mushrooms

1 tbsp shallots, chopped fine

3 tbsp parsley, chopped fine

butter, salt, pepper

Apple-Celeriac Purée

Peel and dice celeriac, potatoes and apples. Put everything in a pot, barely cover with water, season with a pinch of salt, boil until soft and then drain. Return the mix to the pot and allow the liquid to evaporate thoroughly over low heat. Purée everything with a power mixer and pass through a fine sieve. Now add the brown butter and the crème fraîche, season to taste and keep warm.

Preparation

Saddle of Venison

Remove meat from bones, rub in the mix of spices, salt, and brown in hot oil on all sides. Now place the saddle in an oven, pre-heated to 120°C. Remove the saddle after approx. 10 minutes, wrap in aluminium foil and allow to stand.

Cep Mushrooms

Rub cep mushrooms with a damp cloth and cut into slices. Heat some oil and a lump of butter in a hot frying pan, add the mushroom slices. After a short time, add shallots and then season. Carefully add chopped parsley to finish off.

Sauce

Reduce the game stock and port until the mixture adopts an oily consistency. Bind with the cold butter cubes and season to taste with hoisin sauce.

Steigenberger Wine Recommendation 1997 Damilano Cannubi Barolo, Italy

Steigenberger Inselhotel offers guests a front-seat view of Lake Constance. This historic building, a former Dominican monastery and the birthplace of Earl Zeppelin, is uniquely situated on a small private island just in front of Constance. The old part of town, with its winding alleys, magnificent town hall and beautiful town houses, is but a short walk over the bridge from this wonderful luxury heritage residence.

Pike-perch Fillet under a Herb Crust, served with Pinot Gris Sauce

Ingredients

4 small pike-perch fillets

100 g butter

1 egg yolk

1 tbsp each of chives, chervil, dill, flat-leaf parsley, chopped

salt, lemon

125 ml cream

250 ml Pinot Gris

2 cl Noilly Prat

40 g cold butter

1 onion, diced

1 bay leaf

Portion the pike-perch fillet, season, brown and keep warm. Beat the butter until fluffy, add egg yolk and chopped herbs, spread this butter mix on the browned fillets and finish cooking beneath the oven grill until the butter browns.

Preparation

Reduce by half approx. 200 ml of the Pinot Gris with the bay leaf and 1 tbsp of diced onions, then pass through a sieve. Add the cream, the rest of the Pinot Gris and the Noilly Prat. Bring briefly to boil, then stir in the cold butter (approx. 2 to 3 tbsp) until the sauce binds. Season to taste with a little salt and lemon. Serve with potatoes and vegetables of your choice.

Steigenberger Wine Recommendation

2003 Neuweierer Mauerberg, Riesling Kabinett, Baden, Germany

Steigenberger will be opening an unusual hotel in the South Tyrolean health and holiday resort of Merano, on the southern slopes of the Alps, in spring 2006 – Steigenberger Hotel Therme Meran. Under the aegis of Italian star designer Matteo Thun, an imaginative and exclusive 139-room four-star hotel is being created to meet the needs of wellness, holiday and conference guests all in equal measure. The gastronomic portfolio is also an attraction, featuring a blend of Mediterranean cuisine, international highlights and erstwhile Austrian specialities. The buzz of activity in the show kitchen can be observed from both the excellent Buffet Restaurant (seats 208) and the true gourmet restaurant (seats 88).

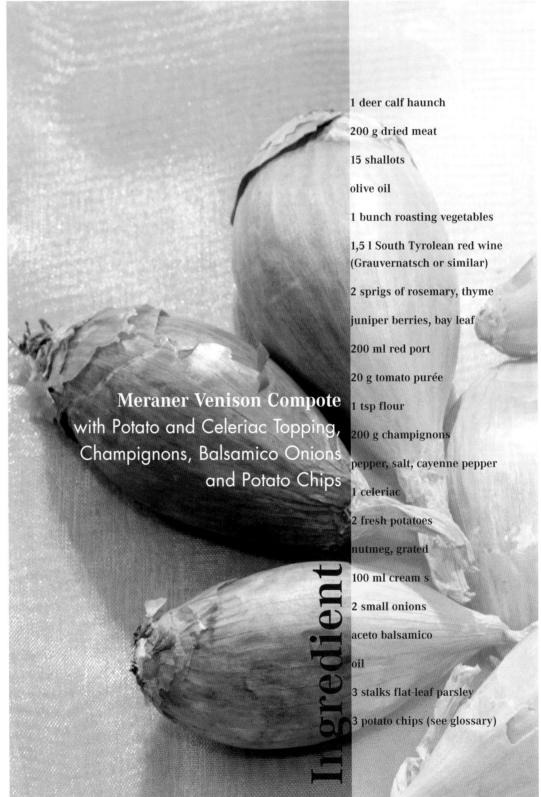

Meraner Venison Compote
with Potato and Celeriac Topping, Champignons, Balsamico Onions and Potato Chips

Ingredient

1 deer calf haunch

200 g dried meat

15 shallots

olive oil

1 bunch roasting vegetables

1,5 l South Tyrolean red wine (Grauvernatsch or similar)

2 sprigs of rosemary, thyme

juniper berries, bay leaf

200 ml red port

20 g tomato purée

1 tsp flour

200 g champignons

pepper, salt, cayenne pepper

1 celeriac

2 fresh potatoes

nutmeg, grated

100 ml cream s

2 small onions

aceto balsamico

oil

3 stalks flat-leaf parsley

3 potato chips (see glossary)

Peel the small onions and marinate in oil and aceto balsamico for 24 hours. Remove the bone from the venison haunch, remove any sinews and cut the meat into small, nutmeg-sized cubes, briefly sweat shallots and dried meat in oil in a roasting pot, add small diced roasting vegetables and sear.

Add tomato purée and flour, sear, and then pour in red port and a bottle of red wine. Allow to simmer. Sear the venison cubes in oil, a few at a time, in a separate pan and add to the roasting pot each time. Add juniper berries, rosemary, thyme and bay leaf and braise in the oven for approx. 1 hour at 200°C (fan setting). Briefly brown champignons and balsamico onions in a little of the red wine gravy, then add to the roasting pot. Place the pot back inside the oven for a further hour until the meat almost disintegrates. Cut celeriac and potatoes into small pieces, season to taste with salt, pepper and grated nutmeg and allow to simmer in the cream until everything is soft. Then purée the mix.

Serving suggestion: place the serving ring in the middle of a pre-heated plate. Fill in venison compote half way up and press on so that the mixture can hold its own. Now top up with the potato and celeriac purée and smooth the surface. Top with the chips. Place the champignons and the balsamico onions around the ring and nap (see glossary) with cream. Sprinkle flat-leaf parsley all around the ring and now carefully remove, taking care the dish does not disintegrate. Serve.

Preparation

Steigenberger Wine Recommendation
2001 Il Futuro, Il Colombaio di Cencio, Gaiole, Chianti, Italy

Steigenberger Hotel Remarque, Osnabrueck, is a hotel for the connoisseur, where well-being and enjoyment are the name of the day. The be-all and end-all of this four-star hotel is its gastronomic variety: gourmet restaurant Vila Real in the conservatory, where the guest is pampered with Mediterranean cuisine and attentive service of the highest quality; wine outlet Enoteca with its wine seminars and tapas evenings; or restaurant Remarque's food & wine, a creative style mix drawn from Cucina Italiana, Eurasian dishes, classics and trends of wellness cuisine.

Crispy Truffled Filo-Pastry Leaves with Saddle of Rabbit, force-fed Goose Liver and Artichokes

Ingredients

6 rabbit saddle portions, boned

4 strips of force-fed goose liver, each weighing approx. 20 g

2 leaves of Swiss chard, blanched

100 g pork caul

4 mini-artichokes

garden herbs, stalks removed e. g. chervil, tarragon, basil, mixed cress

40 g Périgord truffle

2 leaves filo pastry (Greek pastry dough, available from all well-stocked food shops)

some egg yolk

olive oil for baking

salt, sugar

thyme, rosemary

butter

Farce

100 g turkey breast, finely chopped; 40 g spinach, blanched and squeezed dry; 1 egg; 30 g browned (see glossary) butter, cool, but still runny; salt; pepper; 120 ml cream

To make the farce, purée the turkey meat, spinach, egg, browned butter, salt and pepper in a mixer. Gradually add the liquid cream until the farce is nice and smooth.

Truffle Gravy

30 g Périgord truffle, 20 g butter, 50 ml truffle stock made from reduced truffles, 2 tsp truffle oil, 250 ml chicken or veal stock, salt, pepper

For the sauce, sweat the truffle briefly in a little butter and then add the truffle stock. Add chicken or veal stock and simmer to reduce. Season to taste with the truffle oil, salt and pepper.

Preparation

Filo-Pastry Leaves

Spread farce thinly on Swiss chard leaves and wrap in these the goose liver stripes, seasoned with salt and pepper. Slit rabbit saddle portions lengthways, flatten slightly and then also spread thinly with farce. Top with the goose liver chard parcels, roll up and wrap in a minimum of pork caul.
Brush filo pastry with egg yolk. Slice truffle and place the slices on the pastry, then cover again with filo pastry. Cut out squares, each side measuring approx. 5 cm and bake in the oven in hot olive oil at 220°C for approx. 2 to 3 minutes, until golden.
Clean and halve the mini-artichokes and fry in olive oil with a little thyme and rosemary. Fry the rabbit saddle portions in butter until lightly done. Marinate the garden herbs with salt, sugar and a little oil. Serve the halved mini-artichokes and the truffled filo-pastry leaves together with the rabbit saddle portions.

**Steigenberger
Wine Recommendation**
1999 Byron, Pinot Noir,
Santa Maria Valley,
California, USA

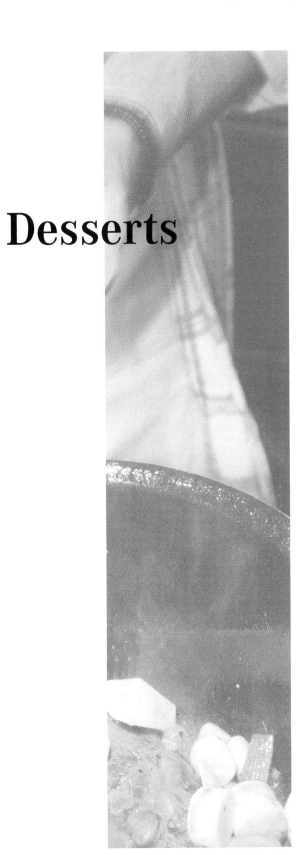

Desserts

| Steigenberger Badischer Hof, Baden-Baden | Steigenberger The Cookbook Fruits of the Forest Terrine wrapped in a Pyramid Cake Shell |

76

Within the walls of a former Capuchin monastery, Steigenberger Badischer Hof in Baden-Baden has been a meeting place for international clientele since the beginning of the 19th century. Entering this stylish hotel, the guest is struck by its welcoming atmosphere and warmth, its balanced mix of historic and modern. Surrounded by its own green park, various thermal pools and wellness facilities feature everything needed for forgetting the stress of a busy day.

Fruits of the Forest Terrine wrapped in a Pyramid Cake Shell

Ingredients

200 ml cream

100 g berries

4 leaves of gelatine

40 g sugar

2 cl raspberry brandy

1 dash lemon juice

4 pyramid cake shells (available from any well-stocked delicatessen)

vanilla sauce (see glossary)

strawberries

Preparation

Soak the gelatine in water. Beat cream and sugar, then add lemon juice and raspberry brandy. Purée the berries with a power mixer and fold under the cream. Carefully fold in the dissolved gelatine and fill the mixture into the pyramid cake shells. Place in the fridge to cool.

The terrine must be allowed to cool for at least one hour before it can be turned out and served. Garnish with strawberries and vanilla sauce.

Steigenberger Wine Recommendation 2001 Sasso Doro, Vin Santo di Chianti Classico, Il Colombaio di Cencio, Gaiole, Chianti, Italy

In the Ahr river valley, Germany's most northerly red wine growing region, lies Bad Neuenahr-Ahrweiler with its magnificent white 19th century buildings, historic half-timbered houses and cosy wine bars. The Steigenberger Hotel, one of the most architecturally refined buildings in Bad Neuenahr, is situated in the town centre right next to the Ahr river, opposite the casino. Be it relaxing in the adjacent wellness centre or conferencing in the convention facility that accommodates up to 800 – this attractive hotel has something for everyone.

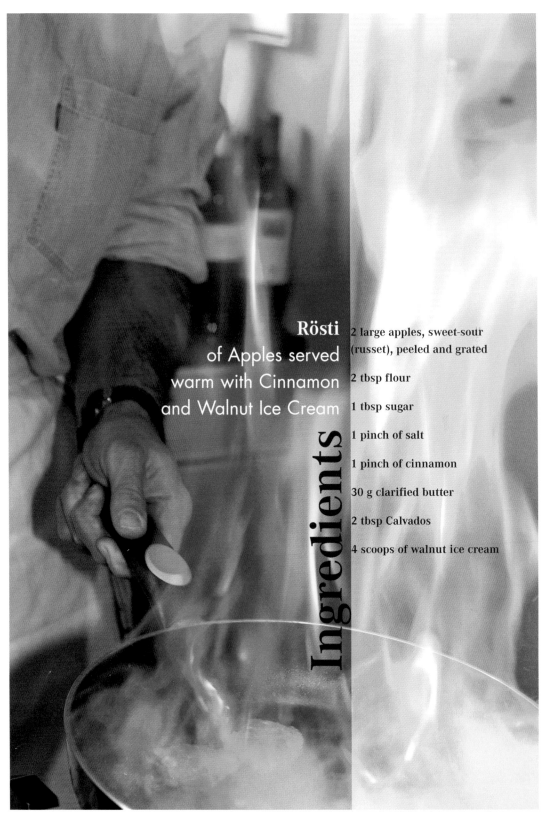

Rösti
of Apples served warm with Cinnamon and Walnut Ice Cream

Ingredients

2 large apples, sweet-sour (russet), peeled and grated

2 tbsp flour

1 tbsp sugar

1 pinch of salt

1 pinch of cinnamon

30 g clarified butter

2 tbsp Calvados

4 scoops of walnut ice cream

Preparation

Mix the grated apples with flour, sugar, salt and cinnamon.

Form small dumplings (approx. 1 heaped tbsp each) and fry briefly in a pan with clarified butter over medium heat.

Press flat to make rounds (approx. 1 cm thick) and continue to fry, turning after approx. 2 minutes and then frying for a

further 2 minutes. To finish off, add a dash of Calvados to the pan and flambé. Serve with walnut ice cream.

Steigenberger Wine Recommendation

2003 Walporzheimer Gärkammer, Spätburgunder Auslese dry,

Weingut Adeneuer, Ahr, Germany

The history of the unusual spa town of Bad Orb, now one of the top health spas, began in 1837, when pharmacist Leopold Koch founded the first saltwater baths in the town. Salt water, health and wellness are also in focus at the Steigenberger Hotel Bad Orb. Besides the classic thermal saltwater baths, numerous health options await the guest in the adjacent spa treatment centre as well as in the Bionouvelle Beauty Centre, which offers a holistic beauty programme designed to treat body, mind and soul.

Strawberry Charlotte
with fresh Fruits of the Forest

Ingredients

4 leaves gelatine

100 g strawberries

170 ml cream

170 ml milk

2 egg yolks

50 g sugar

1 vanilla pod

4 ladyfingers

4 mint leaves

4 tsp icing sugar

fruits of the forest for garnishing

Line small moulds or a soufflé dish with ladyfingers. Soak the gelatine in water and purée the strawberries with a power mixer. Whip the cream until stiff. Bring the milk to boil with a vanilla pod. Beat egg yolk and sugar until fluffy, add the milk and then beat over boiling water until the mixture covers the back of a wooden spoon and forms a rose-like pattern when blown.

Add the gelatine and stir the mixture slowly until cool. Add the whipped cream and the strawberry purée just before the mixture solidifies. Now spoon everything into the prepared moulds and leave to cool in the fridge. Once the mixture has cooled and set, turn out. If a large dish has been used, portion out with a spoon. Garnish with the fresh fruits of the forest, some whipped cream and the mint leaves and dust with icing sugar.

Preparation

Steigenberger Wine Recommendation

Henriot Champagne Brut Souverain, Champagne, France

82

Steigenberger Hotel Axelmann-stein in Bad Reichenhall is one of the most sparkling spa and holi-day venues in the Bavarian Alps. With its stylish ambience, this traditional first-class hotel offers almost unlimited opportunities for relaxing and recuperative spa holidays, as well as for sporting challenges. The tennis courts and a putting green in the spacious hotel park are an invitation to enjoy leisure activities, and the beauty farm, baths and massage centre are there to coddle the guest, as is the in-house Aslan Health Centre.

Soufflé
of Soft Goat's Cheese

Ingredients

2 egg yolks

20 g sugar

20 g fresh goat's cheese

60 g curd cheese

3 egg whites

40 g sugar

20 g flour

some wheat powder

Preparation

Beat egg yolks and sugar until fluffy.

Mix fresh goat's cheese and curd cheese with some wheat powder, ending up with a smooth mixture

that is neither too thick nor too thin. Add the egg-yolk-sugar mix. Beat egg whites and sugar

until very stiff and carefully fold under the cheese mixture. Dust with flour and fill into little moulds

that have been greased with butter and sprinkled with sugar. Bake at 200°C for approx. 20

to 25 minutes.

Steigenberger Wine Recommendation

2004 Winninger Röttgen, Riesling Auslese, Freiherr von Heddesdorff, Winningen,

Mosel, Germany

84

The Steigenberger Airport Hotel at Frankfurt Airport is the place where the whole world meets. Travellers from every country under the sun prize this lively business hotel as a true retreat from travel and business stress. The avant-garde atmosphere of the luxurious spa facilities with a view over the airport's departure and arrival runways, the above average sized conference and congress rooms – everything appeals to the international traveller everyday anew. Four restaurants provide wide culinary diversity – from fine dining to local Frankfurt cuisine. The gourmet restaurant Faces, for instance, serves unusual dishes with an Asian touch in an excitingly furnished interior. The Steigenberger Airport Hotel is a world of its own.

Chocolate Espuma with Mint Jelly
and fresh Fruits of the Forest

Ingredients

200 ml milk

200 ml cream

240 g milk chocolate

120 g sugar

4 leaves of gelatine

2 cl chocolate liqueur

80 g raspberries

80 g bilberries

80 g blackberries

1 bunch mint

100 g mint jelly

Preparation

Dissolve gelatine in water. Bring milk, cream and sugar to boil, dissolve the chocolate in this and then carefully fold

under the gelatine. Stir the mixture and stand in a cool place. Later on, fill into the espuma dispenser (see glossary)

and allow to stand in the fridge. Wash and clean the fruits of the forest and turn in sugar.

Use the espuma dispenser to make the foam (alternatively, beat to a foam in a mixer) and serve the espuma in a

glass. Carefully top the espuma with mint jelly and the sugared berries, top up with chocolate liqueur and garnish

with fresh mint.

Steigenberger Wine Recommendation

Hennessy Fine de Cognac (VSOP)

Steigenberger Hotel Metropolitan Frankfurt, with its historic facade, is located in one of the world's foremost financial centres, popularly known as "MAINhattan". Combining innovative functionality and refined elegance with modern design elements, the hotel creates an atmosphere of well-being. Centrally located right at the heart of the city of Frankfurt, the trade fairs, banking district and historical sights are all within quick and easy reach of the eminent Steigenberger Hotel Metropolitan.

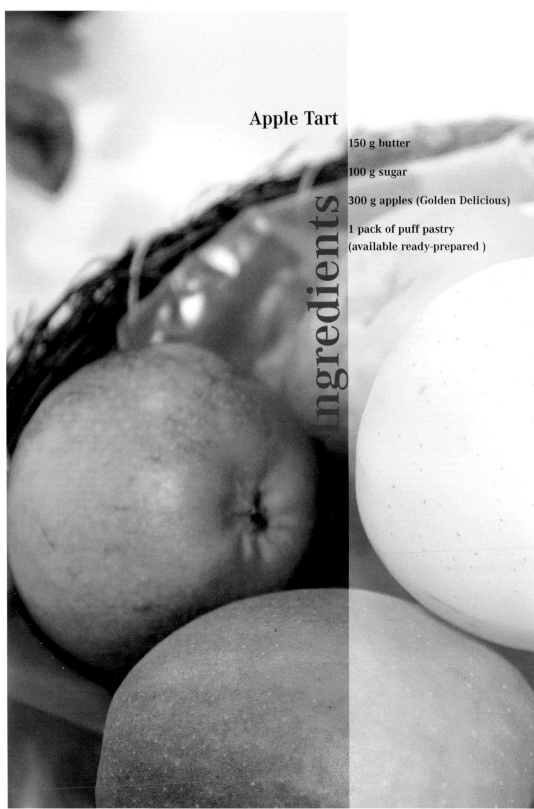

Apple Tart

150 g butter

100 g sugar

300 g apples (Golden Delicious)

1 pack of puff pastry
(available ready-prepared)

ingredients

Put 100 g of butter flakes into a cast-iron pan (approx. 18 cm diameter) and sprinkle with 50 g of sugar. Peel apples, core, cut into quarters and pack into pan. Sprinkle with the remaining sugar, melt the left-over butter and pour over the apples. Cook over medium heat for 10 minutes: the sugar at the bottom of the pan should caramelise but remain light-brown. Cut the puff pastry to the size of the pan base on a lightly floured surface.

Place the pastry circle over the apples and press the edge inwards all round the pan rim. Prick with a fork. Bake the tart in a pre-heated oven at 180°C for 15 minutes. Turn out the tart onto a platter whilst still warm. The tart goes best with vanilla ice cream and whipped cream.

Preparation

Steigenberger Wine Recommendation 1998 Veuve Clicquot Rich Reserve

Set amidst the typical "Bodden", or shallow bay landscape, on the edge of the Jasmund National Park lies a truly idyllic destination for sports fans and nature-lovers: the Steigenberger Resort Hotel Ruegen, with its lovingly renovated manor house, its modern wing and holiday village, leaves no (holiday) wish unfulfilled. Ideally situated for exploring the island interior, this is a perfect family, holiday and wellness hotel, equipped with a beauty and wellness center as well as with the lavish Jasmund Thermal Spa with its giant slide and Kids' Club.

Sea Buckthorn Mousse
with Plum Sauce

Ingredients

200 g white chocolate

6 cl advocaat

200 ml sea buckthorn syrup (available from health-food shops)

30 g vanilla sugar

5 egg yolks

5 egg whites

50 g sugar

150 ml cream, freshly whipped

3 leaves white gelatine

100 ml plum juice

3 tbsp plum purée

Dissolve the chocolate in a bain-marie. Dissolve the gelatine in water. Stir the advocaat and the sea buckthorn syrup into the melted chocolate. Beat the egg yolks with the vanilla sugar until fluffy and the sugar has dissolved completely. Beat the cream and the egg whites separately until stiff, then add the dissolved gelatine. Stir the dissolved chocolate into the fluffy egg-yolk mixture, then fold under the beaten cream, followed by the stiffly beaten egg whites. Pour into an oblong mould and allow to set in the fridge for 2 to 3 hours. Cover the mousse with clingfilm.

Stir plum juice into plum purée. Using two spoons, form the mousse into dumplings and serve with the plum sauce.

Steigenberger Wine Recommendation 1997 Barolo D.O.C.G.
Riserva Castello, Cantina Terre del Barolo, Piemont, Italy

Herb Dumplings

**900 g potatoes, mealy;
120 ml milk; 20 g butter;
80 g flour; 2 eggs; fresh
herbs, chopped; salt;
pepper; nutmeg**

Boil peeled potatoes and press through a potato ricer. Boil up milk and butter, sieve in flour and stir in the eggs. Add this mix to the riced potatoes and season with salt, pepper and grated nutmeg. Flavour with fresh, chopped herbs. Using a spoon, cut out dumplings and either bake in the oven at 180°C (fan setting) or deep-fry in the fryer.

Saddle of Veal

Cut open the veal saddle lengthways and stuff with Serrano ham and taleggio. Roll up, tie up and sear in the pan. Finish cooking in the oven at medium heat for approx. 25 minutes. Pour red wine and port into pan residues and glaze with cold butter (see glossary). Clean and slice cep mushrooms and fry in olive oil.

Steigenberger Wine Recommendation 2004 von Buhl, Riesling Kabinett dry, Reichsrat von Buhl, Deidesheim, Pfalz, Germany

Champagne Sorbet

200 ml champagne, 100 g marzipan, 80 g sugar and some salt, juice of one lemon, 4 blackberries for garnishing

Bring all ingredients, apart from the champagne, to the boil and then deep-freeze in an ice cream maker or in the freezing compartment. Gradually add the champagne.

Biscuit Mix

100 g marzipan, 60 g icing sugar, 30 g flour, 1 egg white

Make a smooth mixture of all the ingredients and form into any desired shape. Bake at 180°C.

Preparation Dessert

International, exclusive, stylish – true of winter sports venue Davos and true of the Davos Steigenberger Belvédère. This five-star grand hotel, built in 1875, joins a grandiose past to a lively present, excelling in terms of unobtrusive elegance, attentive service and perfect hospitality. Once a year, the Steigenberger Belvédère is home to the renowned World Economic Forum, hosting prominent visitors from all over the world. A particularly appealing feature of the hotel is its completely redesigned wellness facilities which offer everything active relaxation requires, from swimming pool to saunas, to massage and fitness rooms.

Carpaccio
of home-marinated Char Fillet
with black Truffles
and Pesto, served with Salads

Davos milk-fed Lamb
served with Mountain Thyme Gravy,
on a weave of grilled Courgettes
with creamed Polenta
and glazed Carrot Pearls

Oven-fresh
Bilberry Jalousie
with Vanilla-Woodland Honey
Ice Cream and Cherry Liqueur
Brandy Zabaione

Ingredients

Milk-fed Lamb

400 g lamb carré

salt, freshly milled pepper
and olive oil

2 sprigs of thyme

2 cloves of garlic

100 ml mountain thyme stock
(see glossary)

Salad Dressing

**2 tbsp white aceto balsamico,
6 tbsp extra virgin olive oil,
truffle oil to taste, beef stock
(see glossary), salt, freshly
milled pepper**

Stir together white aceto balsamico, salt and olive oil, add
beef stock and season to taste
with truffle oil and freshly milled
pepper.

Preparation Hors d'oeuvre

Char

**350 g char fillet, trimmed off skin; 40 g pesto (see glossary); 12 g black truffle, fresh; 100 ml beef stock
(see glossary); salt; freshly milled pepper; 250 g different kinds of green salad in season**

Trim the char fillets of their skin and place next to each other on a piece of clingfilm (depending on the thickness
of the fillets, flatten out slightly with the balls of the thumb and shape all round). Spread the fresh pesto thinly and
evenly over the fillets, cut the black truffle into thin slices and arrange on the fillets. Using the clingfilm, roll up the
fillets and freeze in the deep-freeze. Before serving, allow the char fillets to defrost slightly and cut into thin slices.
Serve with a variety of green salads.

Foto: Deutsche See

Steigenberger Golf Resort El Gouna, the five-star complex opened in Egypt in 1999, is situated on a 36,000 m² peninsula with its own lagoon beach and golf course, at one of the most beautiful holiday destinations on the Red Sea. The hotel complex was designed by award-winning architect Michael Graves. A combination of Moorish style elements and modern design, the buildings merge harmoniously into the lagoon landscape. The predominant shades of earth and sand mirror the typical light and mood of the desert.

Tabouleh

Fried Red Mullet Fillet
with Karkade and Lime-Butter Sauce, Green Asparagus Tips and Fettuccine

Um Ali

Ingredients

Red Mullet Fillet

8 red mullet fillets with skin but bones removed

100 ml karkade
(strong mallow/hibiscus tea – an Egyptian specialty)

100 ml white wine

50 g shallots

50 ml lime juice

100 g cold butter

50 ml cream, whipped

1 tbsp sugar

20 green asparagus tips

200 g fettuccine

Tabouleh

200 g bulgur wheat (see glossary);
500 ml cold water; 5 bunches of
parsley, chopped; 1 bunch of
spring onions, finely chopped;
1 bunch peppermint, finely chopped; 60 ml olive oil; 2 tbsp lemon
juice; 1/2 tbsp salt; 1/2 tsp freshly
milled black pepper; 2 ripe
tomatoes; fresh green salad leaves;
60 ml lemon juice mixed with
1/2 tsp salt

Soak the bulgur wheat in a bowl
in cold water for approx. 30
minutes. Strain through a strainer,
put bulgur on a cloth and firmly
press out any remaining water. In
the meantime, wash the parsley,

Preparation Hors d'oeuvre

spin dry and remove stalks. Place in the fridge. Put the bulgur wheat together
with the spring onions in a bowl, mix and allow to steep a little. Chop parsley
and mint roughly and mix under the bulgur wheat. Mix olive oil and lemon
juice and stir, add salt and pepper. Pour over green salad leaves and mix.
Peel tomatoes and seed them, dice and mix under the salad. Stand at least
1 hour in the fridge and allow to steep. Serve in a salad bowl with fresh green
salad leaves. Serve the lemon-juice-salt mix separately, so it can be used to taste.

Preparation Main Course

In a small pot, allow finely chopped shallots to sweat a little in some butter, then add sugar. Allow to caramelise for a short time and then pour in lime juice. Reduce, then add the white wine and continue reducing. Pour in karkade and reduce further until only one quarter of the liquid remains.

Cut the remaining butter into cubes and, using a whisk, slowly stir into the karkade sauce. Put in a warm place.

Season the red mullet fillets with salt, pepper and lime juice, lightly dust with flour and brown in olive oil on both sides. Place the fish on a platter and finish cooking in the oven for approx. 4 minutes at 180°C.

Boil the green asparagus tips for 12 minutes, then heat carefully in butter and season with salt, pepper and some sugar. Boil the noodles, then toss in butter and season to taste with salt. Arrange the asparagus, the noodles and the fish fillets on a pre-heated plate. Carefully fold the whipped cream under the karkade sauce and spoon onto the fillets. Garnish with fresh herbs and lime and serve at once.

Steigenberger Wine Recommendation
1998 Gewürztraminer Comtes
d' Eguisheim, Maison Léon Beyer,
Alsace, France

Um Ali

200 g frozen puff pastry; 100 g raisins; 50 g walnuts, chopped; 50 g roasted almonds, chopped; 50 g unsalted roasted pistachios, chopped; 500 ml cream; 600 ml cold milk; 2 tbsp starch; 2 tbsp sugar

Defrost the puff pastry and roll out. Bake in a pre-heated oven (220°) until golden brown. Allow to cool. Break puff pastry slightly and put pieces in a soufflé dish. Mix nuts, raisins, almonds and pistachios and sprinkle over the puff pastry, but keeping back 2 tbsp for the time being. Mix cream, milk, sugar and starch and heat carefully, stirring all the time until the mixture is thick. Allow to cool. 30 minutes before serving, pour the cool mixture over the puff pastry and bake in a pre-heated oven (220 °C) for approx. 20 minutes until the soufflé is slightly browned. Decorate with the remaining nuts.

Preparation Dessert

Guests at Steigenberger Frankfurter Hof can certainly get a taste of the high life. This "First Lady" among Frankfurt hotels has been a byword for luxury and comfort for the past 128 years. Although every modern convenience has long been integrated, the splendour of days gone-by has been carefully preserved in this magnificent, listed historic building. Gourmet restaurant Français, Japanese speciality restaurant Iroha, Oscar's café-bar restaurant and the Hofgarten restaurant cater for the most discerning of palates.

Cox Orange Apple stuffed with Goose Liver
on Shallot Purée

Saddle of Salt-Marsh Lamb

Frankfurt Pudding

Ingredients

Salt Marsh Lamb

800 g lamb carré

olive oil

1 sprig of thyme

1 sprig of rosemary

1 clove of garlic, crushed

2 shallots

500 ml chicken stock
(see glossary)

2 tbsp coarse-grain mustard

10 tomatoes, dried

200 g blue cheese

Cox Orange Apple stuffed with Goose Liver

200 g force-fed goose liver,
100 ml veal stock, 100 g lean minced
pork or veal, salt, sugar, pepper,
1 tbsp sweet wine (dessert wine),
1 tbsp port, 1 tbsp cognac, 4 small
Cox Orange apples, 4 small Swiss
chard leaves

Allow goose liver to marinate overnight in alcohol and spices. Cut the top off the stalk-end of the apples and scoop the apples with a melon scoop, leaving a 1 cm thick shell. Blanch the Swiss chard, cut the goose liver into 4 cubes and wrap each cube in one Swiss chard leaf. Evenly coat the cubes with the lean minced pork or veal and press into the apples. Fill the apples with the remaining farce and top with the sliced-off apple tops. Bake everything in the oven at 180°C for approx. 8 minutes. Afterwards, allow the apples to steep for approx. 5 minutes and then halve them.

Preparation Hors d'oeuvre

Shallot Purée

160 g shallots, peeled; 150 ml cream; 120 g butter; a pinch of salt; pepper

Boil the shallots in salted water until cooked. Pour off the water and add cream and butter, allow to reduce. Finely purée everything with a power mixer and season to taste with the spices.

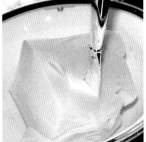

Preparation Main Course

Photo: WMF

Sear the salt-marsh lamb in olive oil, pour off oil and add new olive oil.

Add rosemary, thyme and garlic clove and then roast the meat until pink, fatty side down, in the oven at 200°C

for 7 to 8 minutes. Mix coarse-grain mustard, blue cheese and finely chopped dried tomatoes and spread on the meat.

Place briefly beneath a grill to finish roasting. Allow the chicken stock, two shallots and a chopped clove of garlic to

reduce to a 100 ml sauce. Vegetables of the season make the perfect side dish.

Steigenberger Wine Recommendation Veuve Clicquot Vintage Rosé 1999

Frankfurt Pudding

3 eggs; 75 g butter; 75 g sugar; vanilla; salt; 90 g biscuit crumbs; 50 g almonds, ground; 1 tbsp rum; 1 tbsp kirsch

Separate egg yolks from egg whites. Beat the egg whites stiff with half the sugar. Beat butter and sugar, vanilla and salt until fluffy. Gradually stir in egg yolks, biscuit crumbs, ground almonds, the rum and the kirsch. Fold stiffly beaten egg whites under and fill mixture into little buttered and sugared moulds. Poach in a bain-marie for approx. 22 to 27 minutes at 220°C.

Prepare a fruit purée with fruits of the season, spoon onto 4 plates and place the puddings on top.

Preparation Dessert

Steigenberger Hotel Kaprun is located at the heart of Austria's Hohe Tauern National Park and the European sporting Mecca of Zell am See. This alpine hotel is ideal for mountain fans, nature lovers and relaxation seekers alike. The imposing mountain landscape plus the everlasting ice on Kitzsteinhorn mountain are an open invitation to both mountain walkers and winter sports enthusiasts. Golfers, too, are in their element on the nearby golf course. And, at the end of exertions, the guest can relax in the wellness centre, or with ancient Chinese health therapies, beauty care or massage at the Steigenberger Hotel Kaprun.

Ingredients

Cream of Pumpkin Soup
with Red Pepper Dumplings

Pork Medaillons
with Farmhouse curd cheese Stuffing, served with Beer Sauce and Potato-Vegetable Sauté

Bilberry Turnovers
on Sheep's Yoghurt Sauce

Pork Medaillons

12 pork medaillons, each weighing 50 g

12 slices of raw ham

200 g quark

1 bunch chives

salt, pepper

1 onion

4 cloves of garlic

250 ml beer (Pilsner)

60 g butter

1 tsp caraway, ground

Preparation Hors d'oeuvre

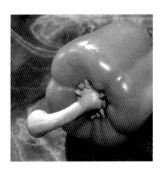

Cream of Pumpkin Soup

50 g honey; 600 g pumpkin flesh;
1 onion, finely chopped; 200 ml
wine vinegar; 250 ml white wine;
2 l vegetable stock (see glossary); 100
g potatoes, mealy, diced;
150 g crème fraîche; salt; pepper

Heat honey in a pot until it goes a
deeper brown. Add the pumpkin cut
into 1 cm cubes plus the chopped
onion and briefly fry. Pour in vinegar
and white wine and add the vegetable stock. Add potatoes and boil
everything for approx. 30 minutes
until the ingredients are soft. Season
with salt and pepper.

Place soup aside, add crème fraîche
but do not return to heat. Purée
everything finely with a power mixer
and then pass through a fine sieve.

Red Pepper Dumplings

1 red pepper, 500 ml water, 150 g white bread (without crust), 1 egg, 2 egg yolks,
50 g butter, salt, pepper

Halve the red peppers, remove stalk and core, cut into strips and boil until soft in
slightly salted water. Drain and pass the pepper strips through a fine sieve, ending up
with a perfect pepper purée.

Cut the white bread into small cubes and mix together with the other ingredients,
add soft butter flakes and allow to steep for 30 minutes.

Now stir this mixture into the pepper purée and allow to rest for further 30 minutes,
but in the fridge.

Using a small spoon, scoop dumplings from the mixture and cook in gently boiling
water for approx. 5 minutes.

Potato-Vegetable Sauté

250 g potatoes, peeled and boiled; 150 g blanched vegetables (carrots, cauliflower, Brussels sprouts, broccoli, French beans); 40 g butter; salt; pepper; some garlic

Slice potatoes and fry until crispy in butter. Cut vegetables into small pieces, add to pan and allow to fry for a brief time, then season to taste with salt, pepper and a little garlic.

Pork Medaillons

Using a slim, pointed knife, cut into the sides of the medaillons (the pocket's cut should not be too large). Season the farmhouse curd cheese with chives, salt, pepper and some garlic. Using a piping bag or a spoon, fill the curd cheese mixture into the medaillon pockets. Now wrap medaillons with raw ham and secure with a toothpick. Briefly brown in a pan and finish baking in the oven for 15 minutes at 180°C.

Remove meat from pan and keep warm.

Using the same pan, now prepare the sauce. Fry the finely chopped onions until brown, add garlic and then the beer. Mix in ground caraway seeds and reduce the sauce by half. Glaze the sauce with the cold, diced butter.

Steigenberger Recommendation Radeberger Pilsner

Dough

500 g boiled potatoes, 150 g flour, 1 pinch of salt, 1 pinch of ground nutmeg, 2 egg yolks

Boil potatoes in their skins, peel, rice and knead together with flour, salt, grated nutmeg and egg yolks
to make an homogenous dough. Roll out thinly (approx. 3 mm) and cut out 8 cm squares with a toothed pastry wheel.
Brush edges with egg yolk.

Filling

250 g bilberries; 40 g icing sugar; 30 g walnuts, chopped; juice of 1 lemon

To make the filling, mix the ingredients and place 1 tsp in the centre of the turnovers. Fold the dough in the middle
and press edges together to make perfect turnovers. Boil in lightly bubbling salted water for approx. 10 minutes.

Sauce

**180 g sheep's yoghurt, 30 g icing sugar,
juice of 1 lemon, juice of 1 orange,
80 g of thick vanilla sauce, 4 mint leaves**

Mix the hot vanilla sauce with the
sheep's yoghurt, icing sugar and orange
and lemon juice in a mixer.

Garnish

**50 g hazelnuts, ground;
2 tsp refined crystal sugar**

Roast hazelnuts briefly in a pan
and mix with sugar.

Preparation Dessert

Why not live like a Guest of State – at least once. Steigenberger Grandhotel Petersberg, also known as the "Gästehaus des Bundes", or "German Camp David", high up on the Petersberg-Plateau, is also accessible to discerning private guests! The hotel stands for exclusive accommodation and exclusive conferencing. But guests can also enjoy a ramble through the Siebengebirge Nature Park or a stroll around the neighbouring city of Bonn's modern museum landscape or around the streets of its beautiful old town quarter. And, afterwards, why not simply relax in this extravagant Grand Hotel's light-flooded wellness facilities?

Iced Foam
of Cucumber
and Aquavit
with fried
Char

Breast and Leg of
Farmyard Duck
with Purée of young tender Peas
and Potato Blinis

Black-Bread Cream
with Ahr Burgundy Sorbet
and Spiced Oranges

Ingredients

Farmyard Duck

2 ducks,
each weighing approx. 2,5 kg

4 onions, 2 apples and
some dried marjoram
for the stuffing

2 bundles vegetables
for soup-making and roasting

2 tbsp tomato purée

400 ml red wine

800 ml orange juice

300 g onions

200 g carrots

4 pieces of spring-roll pastry
(from Asian shops,
alternatively strudel pastry)

Char

4 char fillets, 40 g butter,
320 g cucumber,
40 g yoghurt, 40 ml cream,
4 cl aquavit, 2 leaves of
gelatine, 80 g frisée salad,
40 g rucola, 40 g radicchio,
1 sprig of dill

Purée the cucumber and
pass through a sieve.
Mix the cucumber purée
with yoghurt, cream, dill,
aquavit and a little salt.
Soak gelatine in water,
dissolve and fold into the
mixture. Spoon the smooth

Preparation Hors d'oeuvre

mix into an Espuma dispenser (see glossary)
and put in a cold place. Fry the boned and
salted char fillets in foaming butter. Arrange the
salad on plates and top with the char fillets.

Fill sauce into a bowl and serve separately.

Preparation Main Course

Purée of young tender Peas

800 g fresh peas, 100 ml broth, 40 g shallots, 60 g butter, 1 dash of white port, salt, pepper

Shell half the peas and sweat briefly in a little butter together with the shallots, add broth and cook until done. Put the mixture in a mixer, season, add a dash of port if preferred and mix to a fine consistency. Blanch the remaining peas in salted water, drain and sweat briefly in a little broth and butter, season to taste.

Farmyard Duck

Chop onions and apple and mix with marjoram. Rub salt on the inside and the outside of the ready-prepared ducks, stuff with stuffing and bind. Roast in the oven at approx. 160°C for 45 minutes and then for up to a further 20 minutes at 180°C, if required. Allow to cool and now remove all meat from bones. Halve breasts and cut leg meat into small cubes. Crush the carcasses (see glossary) and brown in duck fat, together with the wing bones and the neck. Add the roasting vegetables and a little tomato purée, continue to brown and then add orange juice and red wine alternately until the gravy has the desired colour (do not allow the ingredients to brown too much as they will otherwise taste bitter). Top up with water and allow to boil for approx. 2 hours, then pass through a sieve. Sweat the leg meat together with finely chopped onions and carrots for a short while, add some gravy and reduce until the result is a compact ragout. Allow to cool. Reduce the remaining gravy to the desired quantity and bind, if wished, with a knob of butter. Spread the ragout onto the spring-roll pastry and form into small rolls. Brush with egg yolk and fry in hot fat before serving. Serve with potato blinis (see glossary).

Steigenberger Wine Recommendation

2002 Dernauer Burggarten, Spätburgunder Qualitätswein medium-dry, Weingut Jean Stodden, Ahr, Germany

Black-Bread Cream

50 g black bread, 4 egg yolk, 75 g sugar, 1 pinch of cinnamon, 4 leaves of gelatine, 2 cl rum, 200 ml cream

Finely grind black bread in a food processor. Beat egg yolk, sugar and cinnamon powder until fluffy. Soak gelatine in cold water, then dissolve in the rum, now fold under the egg-yolk mixture. Carefully fold in the whipped cream and fill mixture into small moulds. Stand in a cool place.

Iced Sorbet

250 ml each of Ahr burgundy and orange juice, 300 ml water, 50 ml lemon juice, 2 cloves, 2 cinnamon sticks, 300 g sugar

Put all ingredients for the iced sorbet into a pot and bring to boil. Allow to cool and freeze in an ice cream maker. If no ice cream maker is to hand, put the mixture into a metal bowl and place in the freezing compartment, remembering to stir the mixture every 15 minutes with a whisk until it has the consistency of ice cream.

Spiced Oranges

4 oranges, 1 vanilla pod, 1 cinnamon stick, 1 clove, 50 g sugar, 1 tbsp food starch, mint, icing sugar

Peel and fillet half the oranges. Press the juice from the remaining oranges and put in a pot together with the vanilla pod, cinnamon stick, clove and sugar. Bring to boil and bind with starch previously mixed with liquid to make a smooth, runny paste. Remove from the heat and add orange segments.

Preparation Dessert

Steigenberger Kurhaus Hotel, Scheveningen | Steigenberger The Cookbook Prawn Salad | Brill Fillet | Marinated Strawberries

116

What started out as a wooden bath house right by the North Sea beach at Scheveningen, seaside resort to the seat of the Dutch government and seat of Dutch royalty, The Hague, has since become Holland's "front parlour" – a truly fairy-tale hotel-palace. Now named Steigenberger Kurhaus Hotel, this edifice makes a wonderful impression with its historic facade and the magnificent paintings in the grand "Kurzaal". For lovers of wellness there is direct access to the "Kuur Thermen Vitalizee", next door, with its modern thermal spa and Thalasso facilities.

Salad of
Prawns
with Beans, Celery
and Nut Oil

Fried
Brill Fillet
beneath a Potato Topping,
with Vinaigrette
and Anchovies

Strawberries marinated
in Aceto Balsamico
with Vanilla Ice Cream
and Vodka Cream

Ingredients

Brill Fillet

4 brill fillets, each weighing 150 g

4 large potatoes, peeled

1 bunch parsley

750 g fresh spinach

10 g anchovy fillets

1 tbsp shallots, finely chopped

1 tsp mustard

5 tarragon leaves

50 ml sunflower oil

50 ml olive oil

40 ml aceto balsamico

50 ml strong fish stock
(see glossary)

Preparation Hors d'œuvre

Prawn Salad

**300 g prawns, 250 g beans, 250 g celery, 1 apple,
8 large champignons, 60 ml walnut oil, 1 lettuce**

Fry the prawns briefly in butter. Season with salt and pepper. Wash beans
and celery and cut into approx. 2 cm long pieces. Peel the apple and cut into
similarly sized pieces – immediately trickle on a little nut oil to prevent dis-
colouration. Remove the peel from the champignons and also cut into pieces.
Blanch beans and celery al dente, drain but do not rinse with cold water!
Now mix beans, celery, apple and champignons with the prawns, add a little
walnut oil and serve.

Preparation Main Course

Brill

Cut potatoes into 3 to 4 mm slices. Now arrange the slices, roof-tile style, over the dry brill fillets. Fry the brill fillets, potato side down, in a hot non-stick pan until golden. Remove from pan and now bake in the oven at low heat (approx. 125°C) for 6 to 8 minutes. To finish off, salt sparingly and brush with neutral-tasting oil.

Vegetables

Sear the spinach together with the chopped shallots in hot oil for a few minutes, then salt and pepper and allow to drain well in a strainer.

Vinaigrette

Remove stalks from the parsley and purée with the fish stock to a smooth mixture. Stir oil, vinegar and mustard together to make a vinaigrette and add a few spoons of parsley purée. Chop tarragon and anchovies finely and mix into vinaigrette. Season to taste with salt and freshly milled pepper.

Steigenberger Wine Recommendation

2002 Chablis Première Cru A.C., Joseph Drouhin, Burgundy, France

Marinated Strawberries

**100 ml aceto balsamico, reduced by half; 2 tbsp honey; 250 ml whipping cream;
500 g strawberries; 3cl vodka; 4 scoops vanilla ice cream**

Wash the strawberries and marinate with reduced vinegar and honey.

Allow to stand for approx. 10 minutes. Whip cream until thick but not stiff

and add vodka. Perfect the dessert with a scoop of vanilla ice cream.

Preparation Dessert

Steigenberger Graf Zeppelin is a hotel rich in tradition. Located in the Zeppelin-Carrés complex in the heart of the Swabian metropolis of Stuttgart, the hotel's atmosphere, its exceptional comfort, excellent service and exquisite cuisine delight even the most discerning guests. Olivio, the hotel's own gourmet restaurant, has already been awarded the prestigious Michelin Star, second time in a row. Steigenberger Graf Zeppelin is a first-class hotel for breaks, meetings and celebrations, and the hotel's in-house Shiseido Day Spa offers ample opportunity to unwind.

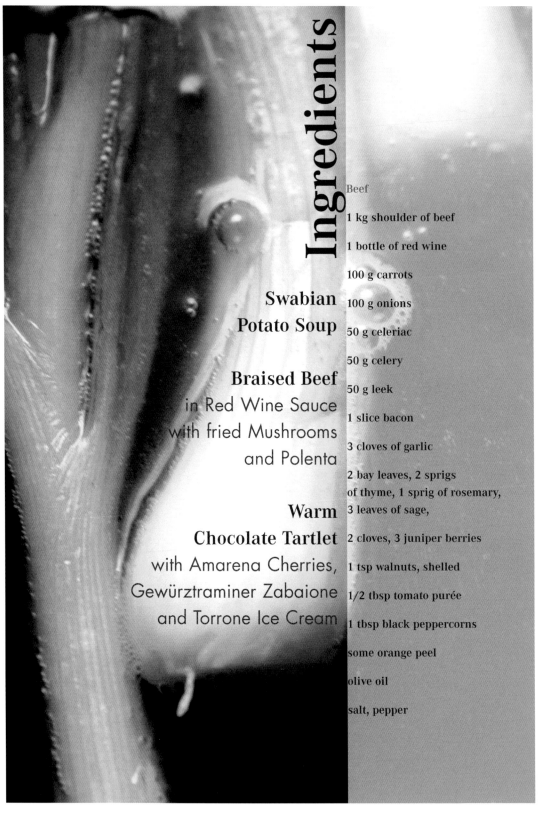

Ingredients

Swabian Potato Soup

Braised Beef
in Red Wine Sauce
with fried Mushrooms
and Polenta

Warm Chocolate Tartlet
with Amarena Cherries,
Gewürztraminer Zabaione
and Torrone Ice Cream

Beef

1 kg shoulder of beef

1 bottle of red wine

100 g carrots

100 g onions

50 g celeriac

50 g celery

50 g leek

1 slice bacon

3 cloves of garlic

2 bay leaves, 2 sprigs
of thyme, 1 sprig of rosemary,
3 leaves of sage,

2 cloves, 3 juniper berries

1 tsp walnuts, shelled

1/2 tbsp tomato purée

1 tbsp black peppercorns

some orange peel

olive oil

salt, pepper

Preparation Hors d'oeuvre

Potato Soup

30 g celeriac; 300 g potatoes,
firm boilers; 30 g bacon; 50 g leek,
diced; 500 ml chicken broth; 2 tbsp
sunflower oil; 1 clove of garlic;
thyme and bay leaf; salt; pepper;
nutmeg; potato chip (see glossary);
chives

Boil the peeled potatoes in salted water until soft, drain and allow to cool. Sweat the vegetables in a pot

in sunflower oil and bacon, not allowing to brown. Add a peeled clove of garlic, thyme and bay leaf

and pour in chicken broth. Add the potatoes. Season with salt, pepper and ground nutmeg. Lightly boil

for 15 minutes.

Remove the herbs and the garlic from the pot and purée the soup with a power mixer.

Garnish with one potato chip and chives.

Mushrooms

300 g mushrooms of the season (chanterelles, ceps, horn of plenty, wood hedgehog); 1 clove of garlic, peeled and chopped; 1 tbsp flat-leaf parsley, chopped; 1 dash lemon juice; 20 g butter; 1 sprig of thyme; olive oil; salt; pepper

Clean the mushrooms and fry briefly in a pan in olive oil together with the garlic. Season with salt, pepper and the chopped thyme. Then add flat-leaf parsley, butter and lemon juice to taste and season once more with salt and pepper, if required.

Polenta

250 ml chicken broth; 1 sprig of thyme; 1 bay leaf; 1 clove of garlic, peeled; 60 g polenta; 30 g parmesan, grated; 10 g butter; salt; pepper and nutmeg

Bring chicken broth to the boil with herbs, garlic, salt, pepper and grated nutmeg, allow to steep for 5 minutes and then pass through a fine sieve. Stir in polenta and allow to boil, stirring constantly, for approx. 25 minutes. Finish by adding the parmesan and the butter.

Preparation Main Course

Cut beef into 2 cm thick slices, season with salt and pepper and fry briefly on both sides in a pan in olive oil. Place the meat in a casserole and cover with red wine, diced vegetables, bacon, walnuts, spices and orange peel. Put the lid on, bring to boil and then braise for approx. 2 hours in the oven (150°C) until the meat is soft and tender. Remove the meat from the pot, pass the gravy through a fine sieve, add tomato purée and reduce. Season the sauce with salt and pepper, halve the slices of meat and return to the sauce.

Steigenberger Wine Recommendation

2001 Nipozzano Riserva, Chianti rufina, Toscana, Italy

Torrone Ice Cream

**3 tbsp almonds and hazelnuts,
40 ml cream, 30 g sugar**

**250 ml cream, 3 egg yolks, 80 g
sugar, 10 g white chocolate, 1 vanilla
pod, coffee liqueur**

Roast the nuts in the oven, caramelise
30 g of sugar in a pot, add the
roasted nuts and pour in the 40 ml
of cream. Allow to boil for 5 minutes.
Spread the mixture on an oiled
baking tray, allow to cool and then
chop roughly.

Bring the 250 ml of cream to the boil
with the vanilla pod. Stir egg yolks
and sugar together in a bowl, pour
the boiling cream onto the egg-sugar
mix. Whilst constantly stirring, heat
mixture in a bain-marie until it has
a creamy, homogenous consistency.
Add the white chocolate and stir
until the mixture is cold. Pass through
a fine sieve into the ice cream maker
and freeze. Just before the ice cream
is ready, add chopped nuts and
a little coffee liqueur.

Chocolate Tartlets

**1 egg, 1 egg yolk, 40 g sugar, 45 g plain chocolate, 50 g butter, 40 g flour, 1 biscuit base,
100 g mixed berries, 16 amarena cherries**

Cut out approx. 4 mm thick circles from the biscuit base, using metal pastry cutters. Place on
a baking tray. Melt chocolate and butter in a bain-marie, stir eggs and sugar together and add to
the melted chocolate. Sift the flour over, put an equal number of amarena cherries on the biscuit
rounds and fill up with the chocolate mixture. Freeze in the freezer for approx. 12 hours. Prior to
serving, bake in the oven for approx. 12 minutes at 200°C.

Gewürztraminer Zabaione

**4 egg yolks, 60 ml Gewürztraminer, 45 g sugar, 1 dash orange juice,
1 dash lemon juice**

Stir all ingredients together and beat to a creamy consistency in a
bain-marie. Serve the baked tartlets together with the Zabaione and
the ice cream.

Preparation Dessert

On the 14th of March 2005, and as part of the ITB, on the occasion of its 75th anniversary the Steigenberger Hotel Group invited prominent guests from the world of hoteliery, tourism and the media to a "Culinary Quintet" at gourmet restaurant Louis in the Steigenberger Hotel Berlin. Five top Steigenberger chefs spent the evening indulging the guests with an unusual anniversary menu: (from left) Holger Zurbrüggen from Restaurant Louis at the Steigenberger Hotel Berlin, Thomas Heilemann from Restaurant Olivo at the Steigenberger Graf Zeppelin in Stuttgart, Thorsten Hopp from Restaurant Faces at the Steigenberger Airport Hotel Frankfurt, Patrick Bittner from Restaurant Français at the Steigenberger Frankfurter Hof and Alfred Schreiber from Restaurant Calla at the Steigenberger Hotel Hamburg.

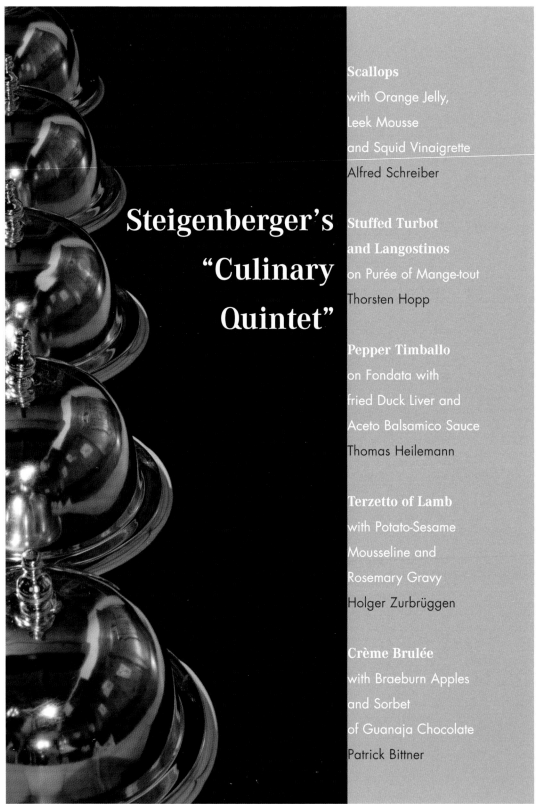

Steigenberger's "Culinary Quintet"

Scallops
with Orange Jelly,
Leek Mousse
and Squid Vinaigrette
Alfred Schreiber

Stuffed Turbot
and Langostinos
on Purée of Mange-tout
Thorsten Hopp

Pepper Timballo
on Fondata with
fried Duck Liver and
Aceto Balsamico Sauce
Thomas Heilemann

Terzetto of Lamb
with Potato-Sesame
Mousseline and
Rosemary Gravy
Holger Zurbrüggen

Crème Brulée
with Braeburn Apples
and Sorbet
of Guanaja Chocolate
Patrick Bittner

Squid Vinaigrette

500 g baby squid; 4 shallots, diced; 1 green pepper, cored and diced; 1 clove of garlic, chopped; 150 ml olive oil; 200 ml white wine; salt

Wash the squid and remove skin (depending on size). Dice and fry briefly in olive oil. Drain. Briefly sweat the shallots together with the pepper and garlic in the remaining olive oil and lightly braise on low heat until soft. Pour in white whine and add squid. Cook on low heat until squids are soft and most liquid has reduced. Add salt to taste.

Orange Jelly

Thinly-pared peel of 6 oranges; 75 ml water; 75 g sugar; 3 leaves of gelatine; 150 ml orange juice, freshly squeezed; salt

Blanch the orange peel in boiling water. Drain. Add the sugar to the water and cook into a syrup, add the orange peel and simmer for 5 minutes. Purée finely, add half the orange juice and bring back to boil. Then pass through a fine sieve. Soak the gelatine in the remaining orange juice and gently heat until the gelatine dissolves, then fold under the purée. Salt to taste and put into small round dishes. Refrigerate for 6 hours.

Alfred Schreiber
Restaurant Calla, Steigenberger Hotel Hamburg

Leek Mousse

500 g leek, washed and with dark green removed; 50 g butter; 50 ml cream; salt; pepper

Halve the leek and wash it. Now cut into thin strips and blanch for 1 to 2 minutes. Squeeze out water and place on a cloth. Bring cream and butter to the boil and season. Now add the leek and cook until soft. Mix everything and pass through a sieve. Refrigerate.

Scallops

8 scallops, shelled and washed; 200 g green asparagus with the lower third removed, and blanched

Place dabs of orange jelly towards the top end of the plate and top with a dumpling scooped from the leek mousse. Cut the blanched green asparagus into strips and arrange in the center of the plate. Fry scallops until transparent, season with salt and pepper. Now place on the asparagus. Pour squid vinaigrette over scallops and serve.

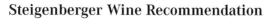

Steigenberger Wine Recommendation

Champagne Billecart-Salmon, Brut Réserve, France

Thorsten Hopp
Restaurant Faces, Steigenberger Airport Hotel, Frankfurt

Cut the turbot fillet in half. Now layer the one turbot fillet with salmon farce, spinach and Parma ham in turns, then cover with the other half of the fillet. Wrap the fish tightly in baking paper, place in a non-stick pan with olive oil and brown at medium heat on both sides for around 2 to 3 minutes. Now place in the oven and finish cooking for 6 to 8 minutes at 150°C.

To make the sauce, peel the shallots, dice and briefly sweat half in butter. Stir in the curry and briefly brown. Then add the vegetable broth. Add the orange juice and the rest of the cream and reduce. Purée with a power mixer, pass through a fine sieve and add salt and pepper to taste. For the pea purée, briefly boil the remaining shallots with the butter, the peas and cream, purée and pass through a sieve. Season with Asian spices if desired. Cut the crust from the herb-bread slices, dry and grate. Turn the langostinos, peeled, in the breadcrumbs and fry in hot olive oil - put in a warm place. Cut the turbot into equal triangles and place upright on a plate. Decoratively arrange the langostinos and pea purée. Foam the thickened curry sauce with the power mixer and decorate around fish.

400 g turbot fillets, 200 g salmon fillets, 200 g Parma ham, 400 g langostinos, 300 ml cream, 100 g spinach, 320 g peas, 250 g shallots, 100 g butter, 200 ml fresh orange juice, 200 ml vegetable broth, 20 g Jaipur curry, 100 ml Calvi olive oil, 3 slices of sliced herb bread, 6 cl Noilly Prat, salt, cayenne pepper

Dice the salmon fillet and blend it with half the cream, the Noilly Prat, salt and pepper in the moulin. Pass through a fine sieve and stand in a cool place. Briefly blanche the washed spinach in hot, salted water and spread on a tea towel.

Steigenberger Wine Recommendation

2004 Grauer Burgunder S, Silberkapsel, Kruger-Rumpf, Münster-Sarmsheim, Germany

Fondata

40 g fontina cheese, grated; 10 g parmesan, grated; 100 ml cream;
100 ml milk; 4 egg yolks; salt; pepper; nutmeg; 1 bay leaf; 1 sprig of
thyme; 1 sprig of rosemary; garlic

Bring cream, together with milk, bay leaf, rosemary, thyme, garlic, salt
and pepper to the boil, then pass through a fine sieve. Add the grated
cheese to the cream, add egg yolks, place in a bain-marie until the mixture
coats the back of a spoon and forms a rose-like pattern when blown.
Then pass once more through the sieve.

Pepper Timballo

3 red peppers; 3 yellow peppers; 300 ml chicken broth; 1 tbsp butter;
1 tbsp flour-butter thickener; 1 tbsp flour; 2 eggs; 2 tbsp liquid cream;
1 tsp tomato purée; 1 pinch peperoncini; 2 small bay leaves; 2 shallots;
150 ml tinned tomato juice; olive oil for braising; 4 x 70 g soufflé moulds;
120 g duck liver; 1 clove of garlic, peeled; 1 sprig of thyme; 20 g butter;
salt and pepper

Halve the peppers, remove cores and ends. Lay the halves on an oiled
baking tray and cook in the oven for approx. 20 minutes at 150°C, cover
with aluminium foil and, once cooled, remove skin. Purée the ends of the
red peppers together with half a sprig of thyme, 100 ml of chicken broth
plus a small clove of garlic. Now do the same with the ends of the yellow
peppers. Pass both pepper purées through a sieve, put in saucepan and

Thomas Heilemann
Restaurant „Olivo", Steigenberger Graf Zeppelin, Stuttgart

reduce fiercely. Put half the shallots in a saucepan with garlic, and lightly braise without browning. Add the yellow peppers, likewise lightly braise
without browning and add salt and pepper to taste. Add one bay leaf and yellow pepper purée plus 100 ml of chicken broth and simmer for approx.
15 minutes. Now remove the bay leaf and purée finely using a power mixer. Season to taste, bind with 1/2 tbsp of flour-butter thickener (see glossary) and simmer 20 minutes more. Lightly braise the remaining shallots in a saucepan together with garlic and the red peppers, season with salt and
pepper, add pinch of peperoncini, bay leaf, tomato purée and tomato juice and cook for approx. 15 minutes. Remove the bay leaf and purée the
mixture with the power mixer. Add 1/2 tbsp of flour-butter thickener and cook 20 minutes more. Allow the pepper mixtures to cool, then heat each
with one egg and a dash of liquid cream in a bain-marie, until the mixtures have a creamy consistency. Then put mixtures into buttered moulds and
poach in a bain-marie at 150°C for approx. 30 minutes. To complete the dish, briefly fry the goose liver with the herbs and garlic. Turn out the red
and yellow pepper Timballo onto the Fondata, garnish with the goose liver and serve with aceto balsamico sauce (see glossary).

Steigenberger Wine Recommendation

2001er „Tasnim" Sauvignon Blanc DOC, Südtirol Alto Adige, Weingut Loacker Schwarhof, Italy

Holger Zurbrüggen
Restaurant Louis, Steigenberger Hotel Berlin

Terzetto of Lamb

4 lamb cutlets; 4 lamb fillets; 120 g boned saddle of lamb; 40 g dried tomatoes; 1 tbsp tomato purée; 1 tsp crème fraîche; 20 g pork caul; 30 g almond semolina; 1 sprig of thyme; 2 spears of lemon grass; 1 yellow pepper; 1 red pepper, 1 tbsp black olives, stoned; 1 tbsp green olives, stoned; 1 sprig of rosemary; 1 clove of garlic; 5 tbsp olive oil; 2 tbsp breadcrumbs; 1 tbsp sesame oil; 1 tbsp sesame seeds; 350 g potatoes, mealy; 500 ml milk; 2 tbsp whipped cream; salt and pepper

Combine the dried tomatoes, the thyme, the tomato purée, the crème frâiche and the almond semolina and purée. Spread the purée onto the prepared lamb cutlets and wrap in pork caul. Bake in the oven for 7 minutes at 200°C then allow to steep for 10 minutes at a lower temperature. Halve the peppers and remove cores. Then salt, and cook in the oven for approx. 18 minutes at 160°C. Remove skin and rub in olive oil. Slightly flatten out the lamb fillets, season with salt and pepper and roll up like a Swiss roll with the peppers. Skewer with the lemon grass then cook in the oven for 7 minutes at 200°C. Finely chop olives, garlic and rosemary and mix with the breadcrumbs. Cut a small round hole in the middle of the lamb saddle and stuff with the olive mixture. Briefly fry in olive oil and place in oven for 6 minutes at 160°C. Allow to stand for 5 minutes. Peel the potatoes and boil in salted water until soft. Drain, pass through potato ricer into hot milk, sesame oil and the roasted sesame seeds. Fold in the cream to finish.

Steigenberger Wine Recommendation
2001 Barba Montepulciano d'Abruzzo, Italy

Crème Brulée

1/2 l milk, 250 ml cream, 2 eggs, 4 egg yolks, 75 g sugar, 2 Tahiti vanilla pods, brown sugar

Bring milk and Tahiti vanilla pods to the boil and allow to steep for 15 minutes, then strain. Beat eggs, egg yolks and sugar until fluffy. Pour vanilla milk onto egg mix and stir well together. Pour the finished mixture into heat-proof soup plates or bowls and cook in the oven for approx. 30 minutes at approx. 90°C. Then stand in a cool place. Prior to serving, sprinkle the brown sugar on top and caramelise under the grill.

Patrick Bittner
Restaurant Français, Steigenberger Frankfurter Hof

Chocolate Ice Cream

5 egg yolks, 250 ml cream, 50 g sugar, 1 vanilla pod, 20 g ginger, 45 g Guanaja chocolate, 1/4 l milk, 10 g cocoa powder

Beat the egg yolks and sugar together with the ginger until fluffy. Put milk, cream, vanilla, cocoa powder and chocolate into saucepan, bring to the boil and stir into egg-yolk mix. Then allow the mixture to thicken in a bain-marie and pass through a hair sieve. Now freeze in the ice cream maker.

Braeburn Apples

4 apples (Braeburn), 60 g sugar, 1/4 l white wine

Quarter and core the apples and cut into small pieces.
Caramelise the sugar until light brown then add white wine.
Now add the pieces of apple to the wine and cook.
When the apple pieces are soft, purée with the power mixer.

Steigenberger Coffee-Recommendation

Alfredo Espresso

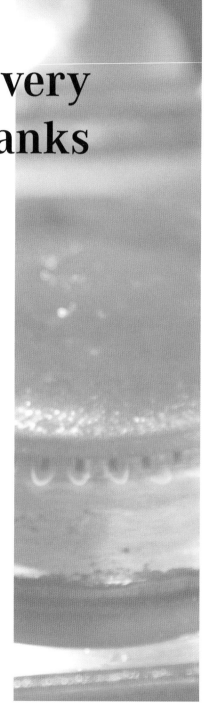

A very
personal word of thanks

It goes without saying that if a meal is to be truly memorable, it must feature a creative recipe, the very best of ingredients and perfect preparation.

The pleasure in producing a special cookbook lies in many ideas collected and in the cooperation of individuals who have contributed their experience as well as their personal tastes to it.

Unique to our cookbook are many recipes from Steigenberger Chefs, who created them and placed them at our disposal with great pleasure and with an astonishing degree of commitment, providing insight into both national and international cuisine, and allowing us a glimpse behind the scenes in their various hotel kitchens. This is the basic bouillon from which the Steigenberger Cookbook has been brewed, and without which it could not have come to pass.

What could two amateur cooks enjoy more than sifting through more than 200 recipes submitted to find the 67 which best reflect the totality of Steigenberger gastronomy? We tried out all the recipes and have presented them for all to understand. The task was to translate recipes from top chefs into a form that anyone can follow, and cook without problems. Both of us used our own kitchens so as to cook the dishes under the same conditions as any normal amateur cook.

We had a lot of fun cooking, tasting, testing, weighing out and weighing up. Sometimes we mulled over if and how this or that recipe is to be understood or how preparing it could be made a delight for all senses. The ever-present dilemma was gauging how many culinary secrets from the Steigenberger kitchens had to be divulged in order to make the book a real experience for the reader.

During the entire process we learned a great deal from each other, and we are already looking forward to Steigenberger Cookbook number two.

A good meal should always be accompanied with a glass of good wine. Wine unites the aromas and rounds the whole thing off. Whilst preparing the cookbook we drank and tasted different types of wine to see which went with which dish, and to pass this on in our wine recommendations.

Godehard Juraschek was the professional in our team. Keen cook, never one to spurn any culinary treat, his role was much more involved than simply taking photographs. He provided much enthusiastic and reliable backup in the kitchen and delighted in our recipe trials as much as we.

For the very best ingredients used in all the dishes we thank our suppliers and partners who helped and advised during the recipe trials.

Whilst the recipe trial cooks were savouring the abundant flavours, Angelika Heyer (Head of Communications at Steigenberger Hotels AG) and her team busied themselves with the editorial side of producing the cookbook. All the recipes were checked as regards clarity of content, layouts were looked at and photographs chosen. Texts were written and edited. Time and again she encouraged us not to rest until the right results were forthcoming from all concerned. Without this crucial contribution, of inestimable value, the cookbook would surely not have become what it is today.

When it then came to artistically presenting the recipes in the book, graphic designer Bobbel Jacobs was called in. She was the perfect compliment to our team, bringing enormous passion to the cookbook's design. The entire layout is the product of her creative muse. It is thanks to her design prowess that the cookbook has a style all of its very own. A lot of hard work was involved, but her fine spirits never left her. We shall miss our midnight cooking chats.

But we should also like to say a very special word of thanks to Vivian and Victoria Steigenberger-Woeller, who, with limitless understanding for the cooking passion and cookbook idea of their mother, not only served valiantly as gastronomic guinea pigs but also went without their own favourite dishes for weeks on end. They were a constant source of encouragement in persevering with this cookbook.

We were very fortunate to have had the support of this team on this project. We would hate to fail to mention any of those who have either directly or indirectly contributed to the success of our cookbook. We sincerely want to thank each and every one of you for the commitment that has made it possible to bring to life the dream of Egon Steigenberger, as well as our own long-held desire – Steigenberger The Cookbook.

For us it has been a wonderful endeavour and adventure, a pleasure for all the senses.

Thank you all again, and from the bottom of our hearts – a time we shall never forget.

Christine Steigenberger und Mike Meyer-Ditandy

Glossary

Conversion Table for Metric and U.S.

Conversion Formulas

To Convert	Multiply	By
g (Grams) to Ounces (1000 g = 1 kg)	Grams	0.035
Liters to U.S. Quarts	Liters	0.95
ml (Milliliters) to liquid Ounces (1 cl = 10ml, 1 dl = 100 ml)	ml	0.030
Celsius to Fahrenheit	Celsius	9/5 + 32

Approximate Metric/ U.S. Equivalents · Oven Temperature Equivalents

Metric	U.S.	Celsius	Fahrenheit
1 ml	1/4 teaspoon	100	210
2 ml	1/2 teaspoon	120	250
5 ml	1 teaspoon	150	300
15 ml	1 tablespoon	160	320
60 ml	1/4 cup	180	355
120 ml	1/2 cup	200	390
160 ml	2/3 cup	210	410
240 ml	1 cup	220	430
1 l	1 Quart		

Al dente

Italian term for pasta which is cooked but still firm.

Amuse-bouche

Small appetizer.

Bake blind

To pre-bake a short pastry without filling.
Line pastry base with grease-proof paper and fill with dried
pulses to keep the pastry base from rising.

Barding

To cover with slices of bacon and bind with kitchen thread.

Blanch

To dip vegetables very briefly into fiercely boiling water and then
immediately quench in cold water. This preserves the colour.

Bind

To thicken a sauce by adding flour or potato starch.

Bouquet garni

Small bouquet of herbs – parsley, thyme, bay leaf,
perhaps other herbs and even vegetables, depending on the dish.

Braising

To briefly braise or brown in hot fat, add liquid and finish cooking
in a covered saucepan.

Brunoise

Finely diced vegetables.

Bulgur

Cracked, parboiled wheat, similar to couscous.

Candying

To replace the water content of fruit with a sugar solution.

Carcass

The bones of small creatures, normally birds or crustaceans.

Chartreuse

1) French herb liqueur, 55% vol. alcohol.

2) Line small moulds or a soufflé dish with finely diced vegetables,
pack with meat farce, add diced game, veal sweetbreads or
similar, top with farce, cover with thin slices of bacon and cook
in a bain-marie (Carthusian dish).

Clarify

To remove particles from a liquid.

Confit

Preserves.

Crèpinette

Minced pork sausage in pork caul.

Croutons

Small, golden-brown bread cubes, tossed in foaming butter.

Espuma

Dispenser in which any type of liquid, combined with gelatine,
can be made into a cold or warm foam.

Farce

A spicy filling for meat, fish or vegetables.

Fontina

Hard cheese from the Aosta valley in the Italian Alps.

Garnishing

Something (such as parsley) added to a dish for flavour or decoration, trimming or adornment.

Glaze

A dish is either brushed with a glaze or is basted with its own fat to produce a glazed surface.

Glazing

To coat a dish with jam and sprinkle it with sugar.

Gratinate

Grilled, browned. Final finish for an already cooked dish achieved by grilling or browning under dry heat.

Gravy

Liquid produced by cooking meat and/or bones, and which has the aroma of the meat. Basic broth for soups and sauces.

Gravy without fat

Gravy without its fat, which sets when cool. Used in sauces and for garnishing cold roasts etc. Sometimes pure meat juice is also referred to as gravy without fat.

Improving

To whisk small amounts of cold butter with a power mixer into a simmering sauce to improve consistency.

Julienne

Very finely sliced strips of vegetable (e.g. carrots, leek, celeriac, onion) that are lightly braised in butter and used as accompaniment or garnish.

Marinade

The spiced liquid used for marinating.

Meat cuttings

Meat offcuts used for making gravies and sauces.

Meat glaze

Broth made from beef, fowl or fish, reduced to a syrup and used to glaze food.

Mousseline

Mousseline farce (a sauce made airy with the addition of whipped cream or beaten egg whites) mixed with jelly is put into buttered moulds, cooked in a bain-marie and served ice-cold.

Mousseline farce

Finely minced veal, fowl or game is cooled well, mixed with salt, pepper, egg white and double cream and used as filling.

Nap

To sprinkle lightly with sauce.

Noilly Prat

French vermouth.

Poaching

Steeping fish, meat, eggs, fowl etc. just below boiling point until done.

Potato Chips

Peel large potato (type that remains firm when cooked), cut into thin slices using mandolin. Deep fry in oil, lay on piece of kitchen roll to absorb fat. Salt to taste.

Pounding

Prior to frying, flatten a slice of meet with the ball of the thumb, gently push together on all sides – makes the meat particularly tender.

Quench

1) To quickly cool cooked food by briefly dipping into very cold water.
2) To pour cold water over a roast to obtain a fine crust.

Reducing

To reduce the water content by evaporation.

Roasting vegetables

Diced vegetables (carrots, celeriac, parsley root, onions) and perhaps a little smoked bacon are roasted briefly in butter with bay leaf and thyme and used as the basis of sauces or meat dishes, or as a piquant extra ingredient.

Rouget

This is the French name for Red Mullet or Barbel.

Roux

Browned flour. Binding agent for sauces. One measure of flour to one measure of butter, slowly heated and stirred.

Saté (Sateh)

Small skewers with marinated diced meat, served with peanut sauce in Indonesian cuisine.

Saucing

To pour sauce over.

Savarin

A yeast cake baked in a ring mould, soaked with brandy or similar.

Sear

To briefly sear in very hot fat to seal the pores, brown and produce the basis of a gravy.

Soup greens

These are mostly carrots, leeks, parsley root and a little celeriac. They are used for flavouring soups, sauces and stock.

Sweat

To lightly fry flour, vegetables etc. in fat, without browning.

Taleggio

Italian sliced cheese, made from unpasteurised cow's milk.

Tranche

A thick slice, a portion.

Trim

Dressing meat or fish.

Trim (pare)

To decoratively trim carrots, potatoes and other vegetables.

Vichyssoise

Originally a potato and leek soup, served ice-cold.

Vinaigrette

Various herbs, finely chopped onions, capers, gherkins, anchovy fillets and hard-boiled egg yolks are mixed with vinegar and oil.

Zabaione

Sauce made of sugar, egg yolk and white wine or brandy or similar (perhaps plus gelatine), beaten to a cream in a bain-marie and mixed with cream.

Dark beef stock (makes approx. 1 l)

30 g roasting fat or dripping; 1,300-1,400 g knuckle of veal or beef shank; 350 g or more beef front shank; 2 sticks of celery, chopped small; 2-3 carrots, chopped small; 2 onions, chopped; 2 leeks, chopped; 2 tomatoes; 2 cloves; 1 sprig fresh thyme; 1 bay leaf; 1 glass red wine, optional; salt

Heat some of the fat in a large pot then brown the bones and meat in it until well browned. Pour fat from pit. Pour in 3 l of cold water and slowly bring to the boil, removing the scum from the surface now and again. Simmer for 2 to 3 hours, always removing any scum. Heat the remaining fat in a pan and lightly fry the vegetables and onions in it. Pour off the fat then add to the stock in the pot the browned vegetables and onions, together with the tomatoes, herbs, spices and red wine, if desired, salt sparingly. Simmer for a further 2 hours (adding the vegetables right at the start will overcook it and make the stock bitter). Strain the stock, cool and skim off the fat. Keep refrigerated.

Light veal stock (makes approx. 1 l)

1,300-1,400 g veal or beef bones, chopped into pieces by the butcher; 350 g front shank of beef; 2 onions, chopped; 3 leeks, chopped; 2 carrots, chopped small; 2 sticks of celery, chopped small; 1 fresh bouquet garni made up of thyme, parsley and a bay leaf; 6 black peppercorns; 1 glass white wine, optional; salt

Put bones and meat into pot and cover with 3 l of cold water. Bring slowly to the boil, removing any scum from the surface now and again. Simmer gently for 4 to 5 hours. If the aroma of the simmering stock is not to your liking, simply bring it to the boil on the hotplate then cover and place in the oven to continue cooking at low temperature. Half way through, add the vegetables, the herbs, the peppercorns, 1 pinch of salt (season to taste again later) and wine, if desired. Pour the veal stock, like the fowl stock, through a strainer, allow to cool, skim off fat and keep refrigerated.

Fowl Stock (makes 1,5 to 2 l)

Carcass of one chicken (or duck) plus giblets, chicken feet or veal bones, optional, chopped; 2 onions or shallots; 2 carrots; 3 leeks, halved; 2 sticks of celery; 1 fresh bouquet garni made up of thyme, parsley and a bay leaf; 6 black peppercorns; 1 glass white wine, optional; salt

Put bones and giblets into a large pot, optionally adding the prepared chicken feet or veal bones. Cover with 3 l of cold water and slowly bring to the boil, removing the scum from the surface now and again. Simmer for 2 to 3 hours, always removing any scum. Add onions or shallots, carrots, leek, celery, herbs, peppercorns and wine (optional). Salt sparingly as the stock will become more concentrated as it cooks and this also intensifies the salt taste. Simmer for 2 to 3 hours (fierce boiling makes the stock cloudy) until well reduced. Remove from hotplate and pour through strainer. If the stock is not to be particularly clear, the vegetables can be passed through the strainer. As soon as the stock is cool, cover and keep in refrigerator or other cool place. The fat that has solidified on the surface can now be skimmed off.

Game Stock

Prepared exactly as dark beef stock, but with game bones instead of beef bones.

Fish Stock (makes approx. 1 l)

Bones and tails of 2-3 sole; 2-3 sticks of celery, sliced; 2 onions, sliced; 1 carrot, sliced; 1 bay leaf; salt

When reduced, fish stock is used as a base for sauces. But aspic can also be made from fish stock and used to coat cold fish. If you are unable to obtain the bones and tails of sole, use the offcuts from aromatic fish such as cod or flounder (avoid flavourful fatty fish, such as salmon). Optionally add 1 or 2 glasses of dry white wine.
Put all ingredients into large pot together with 2,5 l of cold water. Salt sparingly, as the liquid is going to reduce quite a lot. Bring to boil and simmer for 30 to 45 minutes without lid. Put through strainer.

Strong Vegetable Stock (makes approx. 1,2 l)

3-4 large, flat champignons, sliced; 120 g yellow split peas; 120 g barley; 1/2 tsp fenugreek; 1 tsp black mustard grains; 2 tbsp soy sauce; 1 fresh bouquet garni made up of parsley and a bay leaf; 175 ml dry white wine; 1 pinch of sugar; salt and freshly milled pepper

Put all ingredients into a pot (salt sparingly at this stage) and cover with 2,5 l of cold water. Bring to boil and simmer for 1 hour, occasionally skimming off any surface scum. Strain carefully, casting aside the last of the stock as it will be dark and cloudy. Salt and pepper to taste and allow to cool.

Mountain Thyme Stock

Lamb offcuts, 30 g shallots, 2 sprigs of thyme, 3 cl red wine with body, 4-5 white peppercorns, 100 ml meat stock, fresh ice-cold butter

Sauté the lamb offcuts, add chopped shallots, one sprig of thyme and peppercorns. Add red wine, meat stock and reduce to desired consistency, pass through a sieve and season to taste.
Shortly before serving add freshly chopped thyme and bind the stock with ice-cold butter.

Tomato Stock (makes 1 l)

40 ml olive oil, 75 g onions, 15 g sugar, 3 cloves of garlic, 1 kg tomatoes, salt, 1 bay leaf, 1 Swiss chard, salt, pepper

Lightly sweat the finely chopped onions, sugar and garlic in olive oil. Add finely diced tomatoes, salt and bay leaf and simmer for 15 to 20 minutes. Mix, then pass through sieve.

Aceto Balsamico Sauce

Reduce gravy or stock by half, add aceto balsamico, salt and pepper to taste and glaze with a little cold butter.

Frankfurt Green Sauce

1-2 boiled eggs, 8 tbsp of sour cream, 200 g yoghurt, juice of 2 lemons, 300 g curd cheese, 2 pinches of sugar, 240 g mixed fresh herbs (borage, chervil, cress, parsley, burnet, sorrel and chives), 2 shallots, salt and pepper

Put sour cream, yoghurt, lemon juice and curd cheese into basin and stir well together. Add salt, pepper and sugar to taste. Wash the herbs and chop finely. Finely chop the shallots and stir into the sauce together with the herbs. Shell the eggs, dice and add to the sauce. Add salt, pepper and lemon juice to taste.

Red Wine Sauce

2 shallots, 1 clove of garlic, 200 ml port, 200 ml red wine, 100 ml chicken broth, 20 g butter

Dice shallots and garlic and lightly sweat in butter. Add port and reduce. Add red wine and again reduce. Add chicken broth, pass through fine sieve and glaze the sauce with a little butter.

Chive Sauce

1 large bunch of chives, 1 orange, 1 lemon, 100 g yoghurt, 100 g sour cream, 100 g crème fraîche, sugar, salt, pepper, cayenne pepper, vinegar

Mix yoghurt, cream, crème fraîche, lemon and orange juice, add vinegar and seasonings to taste, then purée. Cut chives small and stir in.

Vanilla Sauce

**400 ml milk, 1 vanilla pod, 20 g lemon peel, 3 egg yolks,
125 g sugar, 30 g flour**

Heat milk and add lemon peel and vanilla pod, cut lengthways.
Stir egg yolk, sugar and flour in a bowl until smooth. Scrape
pulp from vanilla pod, remove pod and lemon peel. Stir vanilla
pulp and egg mix into hot milk and cook on low heat until desired
consistency is obtained.

Leek Paste

1 leek, 125 g butter, 1/2 lemon, salt, pepper

Blanch the leek, allow to cool then purée with butter in the mixer.
Salt and pepper to taste.

Flour-Butter Thickener

One measure of flour to one measure of butter stirred to a paste
(beurre manié). For binding soups, sauces, stews.

Browned Butter

Brown unsalted butter in a pan. The browned butter must be
filtered through paper to remove even the smallest milk particles.
Best to put kitchen paper on a fine round sieve and pour butter
through.

Breadcrumb-Butter

Melt butter in a pan, then raise temperature and add finely
grated breadcrumbs. Roast everything, add the crunchy butter
to the finished dish and serve.

Pesto (400 g)

**80 g basil; 1 tsp coarse salt; 30 g pine kernels; 3 cloves of garlic;
40 g parmesan, freshly grated, 20 g Pecorino, freshly grated;
250 ml extra virgin olive oil; freshly milled pepper**

Crush salt, pine kernels and garlic with pestle and mortar,
add basil leaves and crush finely. Stir the two grated cheese
varieties and the olive oil into the mixture to finish off.

Potato Blinis

**7-8 potatoes, 100 g wheat flour, 30-40 g yeast, 4 glasses of milk,
1/2 glass of cream, 5 eggs, salt**

Pour 2 glasses of lukewarm milk into a casserole, dissolve the
yeast in it, add milk and knead into a dough. Cover the casserole
with a cloth and put in a warm place.
Peel the potatoes, boil until done, drain, put through ricer, add
butter and cream and mix well. Mix the well-risen dough with the
potato purée, salt, beaten egg and stiffly whipped egg white.
Then add remaining milk and allow dough to rise again. Fry the
small potato pancakes (blinis) in a frying pan.

Partners

We thank our business partners of many years standing for their cooperation.

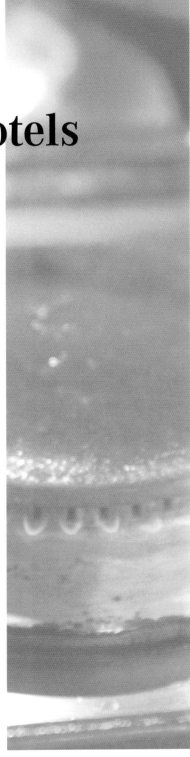

The Hotels

Steigenberger Conti Hansa

Schlossgarten 7

24103 Kiel, Germany

Tel. +49 431 5115 – 0

Fax +49 431 5115 – 444

kiel@steigenberger.de

Steigenberger Grandhotel Petersberg

Petersberg

53639 Königswinter/Bonn, Germany

Tel. +49 2223 74 – 0

Fax +49 2223 74 – 443

info@petersberg.steigenberger.de

Steigenberger Inselhotel

Auf der Insel 1

78462 Konstanz, Germany

Tel. +49 7531 125 – 0

Fax +49 7531 26402

konstanz@steigenberger.de

Steigenberger Mannheimer Hof

Augustaanlage 4-8

68165 Mannheim, Germany

Tel. +49 621 4005 – 0

Fax +49 621 4005 – 190

mannheim@steigenberger.de

Steigenberger Hotel Remarque

Natruper-Tor-Wall 1

49076 Osnabrück, Germany

Tel. +49 541 6096 – 0

Fax +49 541 6096 – 600

osnabrueck@steigenberger.de

Steigenberger Resort Hotel Rügen

Neddesitz

18551 Sagard/Rügen, Germany

Tel. +49 38302 95

Fax +49 38302 96 – 620

ruegen@steigenberger.de

Steigenberger Graf Zeppelin

Arnulf-Klett-Platz 7

70173 Stuttgart, Germany

Tel. +49 711 2048 – 0

Fax +49 711 2048 – 542

stuttgart@steigenberger.de

Steigenberger Strandhotel Zingst

Seestraße 54

18374 Ostseebad Zingst, Germany

Tel. +49 38232 85 – 0

Fax +49 38232 85 – 999

zingst@steigenberger.de

Abroad

Steigenberger Hotel Kaprun

Schlossstraße 751

5710 Kaprun/Zell am See, Austria

Tel. +43 6547 7647 – 0

Fax +43 6547 7647 – 503

kaprun@steigenberger.at

Steigenberger Avance Hotel

Am Goldberg 2

3500 Krems/Wachau, Austria

Tel. +43 2732 71010

Fax +43 2732 71010 – 50

krems@steigenberger.at

Steigenberger Belvédère

Promenade 89

7270 Davos-Platz, Switzerland

Tel. +41 81 41560 – 00

Fax +41 81 41560 – 01

davos@steigenberger.ch

Steigenberger Bellerive au Lac

Utoquai 47

8008 Zürich, Switzerland

Tel. +41 1 254 – 4000

Fax +41 1 254 – 4001

bellerive@steigenberger.ch

Steigenberger Kurhaus Hotel

Gevers Deynootplein 30

2586 CK Den Haag-Scheveningen,

Netherlands

Tel. +31 70 4162 – 636

Fax +31 70 4162 – 646

info@kurhaus.nl

Steigenberger Golf Resort

El Gouna/Rotes Meer, Egypt

Tel. +20 65 5801 – 41

Fax +20 65 5801 – 49

steigelg@link.com.eg

Steigenberger Hotel Therme Meran

Thermenplatz

39012 Meran, Italy

Tel. +39 473 2520 – 00

Fax +39 473 2520 – 22

STEIGENBERGER HOTEL GROUP   **STEIGENBERGER** HOTELS & RESORTS   *InterCityHotel*

The Steigenberger Hotel Group, with registered offices in Frankfurt am Main, runs about 80 hotels under the brand names

"Steigenberger Hotels & Resorts" and "InterCityHotels" in Germany, Austria, Switzerland, Italy, The Netherlands and Egypt.

Imprint

Disclaimer

All information and particulars contained in this book have been produced by the authors, to the best of their knowledge and belief, and checked with the utmost care by the authors and the publisher. As regards product liability law, we would like to point out that errors and omissions in content cannot be entirely ruled out. Neither the authors nor the publisher can accept any obligation or liability as regards any incorrect statements. Suggested corrections are always welcomed and considered.

Publisher

Steigenberger Hotels AG, Lyoner Strasse 40, 60528 Frankfurt am Main, Germany
www.steigenberger.de

Authors

Christine Steigenberger
Mike Meyer-Ditandy

ISBN 3-00-017410-9

1st Edition 2005

Print run

20,000 copies in German
 5,000 copies in English

Printer

Druckerei Schanze Ltd. & Co. KG, Kohlenstraße 132, 34121 Kassel, Germany

Layout

Bobbel Jacobs, Neuhofstrasse 42, 60318 Frankfurt am Main, Germany

Edited and realised by

Team drawn from the Department of Corporate Communication, Steigenberger Hotels AG, Angelika Heyer, Lyoner Strasse 40, 60528 Frankfurt am Main, Germany

Reproduction

Repro 45, Morgensternstrasse 37, 60596 Frankfurt am Main, Germany

Editorial Department

Tanja Reindel, Habsburger Allee 38, 60385 Frankfurt am Main, Germany

Photographs

Godehard Juraschek, Fotografenmeister, Eduard-Berdel-Strasse 20, 56203 Höhr-Grenzhausen, Germany